THE GIFT
OF ANGER

THE GIFT
OF ANGER

USE PASSION
TO BUILD
NOT DESTROY

◇ **JOE SOLMONESE** ◇

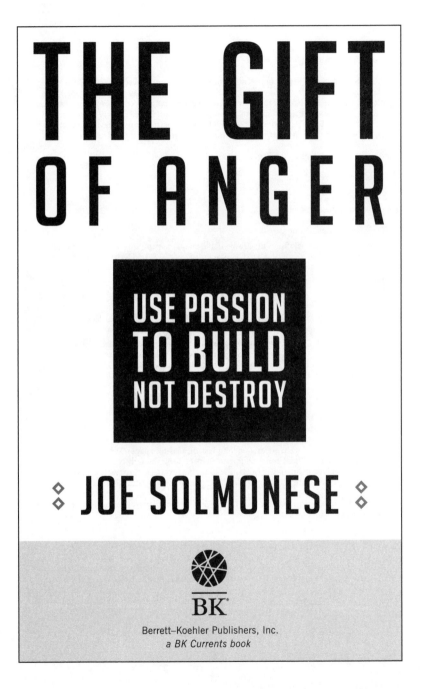

BK

Berrett–Koehler Publishers, Inc.
a BK Currents book

Berrett-Koehler Publishers, Inc.
1333 Broadway, Suite 1000
Oakland, CA 94612-1921
Tel: (510) 817-2277
Fax: (510) 817-2278
www.bkconnection.com

Ordering Information

Quantity sales. Special discounts are available on quantity purchases by corporations, associations, and others. For details, contact the "Special Sales Department" at the Berrett-Koehler address above.

Individual sales. Berrett-Koehler publications are available through most bookstores. They can also be ordered directly from Berrett-Koehler: Tel: (800) 929-2929; Fax: (802) 864-7626; www.bkconnection.com.

Orders for college textbook/course adoption use. Please contact Berrett-Koehler: Tel: (800) 929-2929; Fax: (802) 864-7626.

Orders by U.S. trade bookstores and wholesalers. Please contact Ingram Publisher Services: Tel: (800) 509-4887; Fax: (800) 838-1149; E-mail: customer.service@ingram publisherservices.com; or visit www.ingrampublisherservices.com/Ordering for details about electronic ordering.

Berrett-Koehler and the BK logo are registered trademarks of Berrett-Koehler Publishers, Inc.

Printed in the United States of America

Berrett-Koehler books are printed on long-lasting acid-free paper. When it is available, we choose paper that has been manufactured by environmentally responsible processes. These may include using trees grown in sustainable forests, incorporating recycled paper, minimizing chlorine in bleaching, or recycling the energy produced at the paper mill.

Cataloging data is available from the Library of Congress, catalog no. 2016021766
ISBN: 978-1-62656-588-3

First Edition
21 20 19 18 17 16 ‡‡ 10 9 8 7 6 5 4 3 2 1

Produced and designed by BookMatters, Berkeley; copyedited by Amy Smith Bell; proofed by Janet Reed Blake; indexed by Leonard Rosenbaum. Cover design by Irene Morris Design.

CONTENTS

FOREWORD

My son, Matthew Shepard, was murdered in 1998 in Laramie, Wyoming, simply because of his sexual orientation. He was a caring and selfless young gay man with a bright future. His death brought to the public's attention the horror of violence based on sexual orientation. I was determined that Matt's life and death should have a more lasting meaning. Soon after Matt's death, my husband, Dennis, and I started the Matthew Shepard Foundation, and we have since devoted our lives to ending hate-based violence and passing federal legislation that offers greater protection to LGBTI Americans who find themselves victims of senseless violence.

The process of passing a major piece of legislation was daunting, and the resistance we faced in Congress both surprised and angered us. Yet Dennis and I persevered, working closely with the Human Rights Campaign (HRC) and its visionary leader, Elizabeth Birch. The partnership gave us great hope, support, and the will to carry on. When Elizabeth left her post at HRC, we wondered about the future and what it would mean to our important work. But when Joe Solmonese took the helm, we knew that we had a strong, empathetic, strategic leader and, ultimately, a good friend for life. Dennis and I felt immediately comfortable and confident in Joe. Calm and poised, he had an aura of competence and clarity about the path forward. Confident that this legislation was something we could accomplish, Joe never took his eyes off that goal—not for one day. While he took the work very seriously, he never took himself or his position too seriously.

Some people felt that Joe appeared too focused on the work, on the details of the plan, rather than on expressing his anger, given the gravity of the work. As an introvert, I think his disposition drew us closer. While I had more than enough reason to express my anger as I walked through the halls of Congress, I knew that to do so would likely keep us from accomplishing our goal. I would be lowering myself to the most base of reactionary behavior, and that was something I was unwilling to do. So I kept my anger in check. Recently I was surprised to learn from Joe that it was I, more than anyone, who had inspired him to channel his anger in ways that led to greater effectiveness and, ultimately, to write this book. I had never thought of it that way, but when I reflected back on the many difficult conversations I'd had over the years, the endless insulting, misguided, and erroneous things I had to listen to about our mission, I realized that I too had learned to channel my anger in a way that would create a lasting legacy for my son. With Joe's guidance, patience, and help, the Matthew Shepard and James Byrd Jr. Hate Crimes Prevention Act (HCPA) was passed and signed into law by President Barack Obama October 29, 2009. This legislation has helped millions of people live free from the hate-based violence that our family faced.

Today I consider Joe part of my family. He has been a blessing for me. He navigated the difficult world he found himself in, took the anger he felt at the injustices we faced, and became a thoughtful creator and leader of transformative and lasting change. We all have something to learn from him. I learned from Joe that politics, and accomplishing real change, is a tough and sometimes ugly business. I respect that Joe handled it with such grace. The fact that he is forthright and upfront with people is important and aligns with how I feel about the work that the Matthew Shepard Foundation accomplishes. *The Gift of Anger* brilliantly connects Joe's unique experiences with life lessons that anyone can use. I love his no-nonsense approach to finding common ground and to creating alliances for mutually beneficial results. More important, Joe understands how people think. He shares his perspective on how to get the most positive outcomes in difficult situations. Joe's ability to take the long view is anything but effortless, yet readers will find, as I have, that with careful attention, anything is possible.

—*Judy Shepard*
May 2016

INTRODUCTION

On the morning of December 22, 2010, I found myself standing backstage in an auditorium at the Department of the Interior, waiting for the president of the United States. Barack Obama was on his way to sign into law the bill that would end the discriminatory policy known as Don't Ask, Don't Tell (DADT). For seventeen years, brave men and women who had been serving their country in silence had been fighting to end this ban. As president of the Human Rights Campaign, the largest LGBT civil rights organization in the country, I had the privilege of leading the organization's efforts and working alongside President Obama to get this landmark legislation passed into law. On that historic morning, I would have a few minutes backstage to chat with the president before I took my seat among hundreds of witnesses, including LGBT activists, journalists, bloggers, and service members most impacted by the discriminatory policy.

When President Obama walked in, he came right up to me and gave me a hug. With his hand on my shoulder, he said, "Wow, even I didn't get kicked in the teeth on this one as much as you did. And I'm always the guy who gets kicked in the teeth in tough legislative fights." The bill to repeal Don't

Ask, Don't Tell had come perilously close to failing more than once during the previous few months. As a result, there had been a great deal of anger within the LGBT community—anger that had been brewing since 1993 when DADT had been put in place. More recently, this anger had been directed at me and the other activist leaders who were working hard with the Obama administration to get this bill passed. To be honest, the moment of repeal was bittersweet for me. Even though I was surrounded by people, I was standing alone. The truth was, for the past few months I had spent just as much time responding to negative attacks from my own community as I had working the halls of Congress.

I had heard the anger and frustration from the LGBT community for as long as we had been working toward repeal. However, I was able to dissociate from it because I had a plan: I was resolved to channel my own anger toward a singular strategic end. I always knew that we would prevail, that DADT would be repealed—although I didn't realize it would be just hours before the end of the 2010 congressional session and days before the holiday break. I was aware that not everyone in the LGBT community agreed with my strategy, but luckily there were many people who helped me achieve the ultimate goal. Others expressed their fury in unproductive ways. Although dealing with all of this anger didn't always feel good, and the path forward often seemed confusing and frustrating, my team remained laser focused on the six senators we needed to turn. Our strategy emphasized understanding what was at the heart of their resistance to supporting the bill. We spoke directly to that resistance in an incredibly effective way. Our campaign spoke to *their* concerns, not ours. Ultimately, the plan worked.

Earlier in the day, one of the many LGBT bloggers approached me. He had been unrelenting in his criticism of HRC's work; I believed he was stoking the fires of the community's collective anger to keep his readership up. Instead of congratulating me, he simply said, "Well, you must feel vindicated." Even on this day, when the bill would finally be passed into law, this blogger couldn't let go of his anger. But I wouldn't let him spoil my day. As Marine Staff Sergeant Eric Alva walked onto the stage in anticipation of the president signing the bill, he was beaming. Staff Sergeant Alva gave me the thumbs up, and I saw pure joy on his smiling face. In that moment, I knew that as a community we had channeled our collective anger into something transformative.

During this particular legislative fight, I learned a lot about what worked and what didn't when it came to getting what I wanted for my community and myself. While much of the resistance we face throughout our lives has the potential to make us angry, it's what we do about that anger that determines how quickly and effectively we can overcome the obstacles and get to the place we want to be. Today, more than five years later, I reflect on what I learned about confronting injustice, dealing with the understandable anger that is a valid response to injustice, and channeling this passion toward creating positive change.

I came to public service with a very simple goal: to help people, to make their lives better in significant and tangible ways. I have a record of accomplishments that has helped women, LGBT people, and others who have been marginalized or discriminated against become more powerful both within the workplace and in their individual lives. Whether it's helping to elect people to office who eventually helped to pass the Lilly Ledbetter Fair Pay Act (2009), which states that everyone should make the same amount of money regardless of gender, or the Matthew Shepard and James Byrd Jr. Hate Crimes Prevention Act (2009), which protects us all from violence, I learned that there is a savvy, pragmatic, and replicable way to have your voice heard and get what you want. How was I able to deliver these tangible results, to create such significant social change for all Americans? I relied on fundamental yet profoundly important life lessons that were instilled in me throughout my upbringing as well as during my early years of professional development. In this book I want to share these lessons, so you can create your own moments of change in your personal and professional relationships.

:: ::

I describe my upbringing as relatively average. I grew up in southeastern Massachusetts in an incredibly homogeneous small town. My parents were teachers who belonged to a union: they created a progressive, democratic household, typical of middle-class Massachusetts in the early 1970s. My father, a strict Italian American, died when I was thirteen. After that, my mother raised my siblings and me on her own. Like so many others, for me high school was not the be-all and end-all; I was often sad and scared. Despite being on the track team and in student government and having good friends, like many young gay men, I was occasionally bullied. Some kids would call me names, throw things at me as I walked through the halls, or speak to me in a mocking feminine voice. Although I was never in a situation where I feared for my own safety, I searched for ways to survive and just make it through. In some ways, I relied on the New England sensibilities my parents had instilled in me—suppress your anger, keep a stiff upper lip, be tough, don't let your emotions show.

In other ways, I did what many gay youth still do: imagine a future far away from that high school environment. In my mind the story of my future success would take place in a glamorous, big urban city filled with interesting and diverse people doing interesting and diverse things. I often thought, *Once I get out of here, I'm never looking back. I'll show them who's going to end up the real success story. Someday, I'll get my revenge.* Without really knowing it, I was taking the long view of life. I was also taking the long view with my anger. I had disciplined myself to channel my anger to propel me out of where I was and put me where I wanted to be. I didn't suppress or ignore my anger—I never have—but I've always been very clear about what I've wanted for myself and for the people I've represented. Anger for the sake of anger, or rage that is directed at nothing other than feeling furious, gets you nowhere. I never let my anger keep me from losing sight of the ultimate goal: to get out and to one day make a difference.

When it was time to go off to college, I was attracted to Boston University, drawn to the danger, energy, and excitement of the big city. Boston was nothing like small-town southeastern Massachusetts. I knew that I would meet interesting and diverse people because the *world* goes to school in Boston. It was exactly what I had envisioned throughout those long high school years. BU was the perfect choice for me. I could have come out during college, but I didn't. It wasn't so much that I was hiding; my sexuality was simmering in the back of my mind. I was attracted to men, yet I had a girlfriend. I was trying to fit into traditional male roles that I'd grown up with. I wasn't exactly being true to myself, but I was happy and carefree. For the first time in a long time, I put aside my anger about the occasional injustices I experienced in my own world.

In my junior year of college I landed *the* internship: working in the Massachusetts State House in the Governor's Office, for Michael Dukakis, who was running for reelection as governor with an eye toward a presidential bid. In the governor's scheduling office, as part of his personal staff, I vetted all the invitations that came in for the governor and the First Lady, Kitty Dukakis. I immediately connected with the energy in the State House. I thought it was just the coolest thing in the world. Mike Dukakis wasn't just any governor. He was the progressive governor of a progressive state who was going to be running for president. I was surrounded by amazing, smart, passionate people. Some of them had just graduated from Harvard Law School and could have had any job they wanted, but they chose state government because they believed in reforming the healthcare system or helping to revive the state's economy.

Although I didn't set out to be in public service or to be

a role model or a leader, I found my way in and I embraced it. I worked hard and loved it. I made myself indispensable in the governor's office, and when I graduated from college two years later, they offered me a full-time paid position: sixteen thousand dollars a year. It was like a dream come true. There I learned that power could come with compromise and that being in the center of the activity as an integral part of a team working toward a common goal was inspiring and energizing.

Right about that same time I started focusing on myself, coming into some awareness of who I really was: a gay man. I moved in 1989 into the South End, an almost exclusively gay Boston neighborhood. I reconnected with a hometown friend, Jack Gorman, who introduced me to all of his friends. During those years, if you weren't out at work and you weren't out to your family, there was a tribalness to being gay, where your intimate circle of friends provided all of the support and love that you feared your family might not provide. My neighborhood friends—a group of seven guys—became my tribe. We lived within blocks of each other. We went to work in the morning but talked on the phone throughout the day about our evening and weekend plans. We met at the gym after work, had dinner together, socialized, and made our summer pilgrimage to Provincetown (a coastal Massachusetts vacation destination for the LGBT community). If someone in our tribe didn't have money, someone else lent them money; if one of us didn't have a place to live, the tribe would offer shelter. I felt unconditional acceptance and support, empowered to be out at work and out at home. These days were a joyous celebration: I finally felt like I belonged.

:: :: :: ::

Then there was AIDS. AIDS changed everything for us. For the first time in a long while, I felt anger but also fear. I was just embarking on a new chapter in my life, happily living as an openly gay man, and the AIDS epidemic was affecting everyone I knew and cared about. I became very committed, as most people in the LGBT community were, to raising both awareness and money to support the fight. I came to understand the greater importance of my work in public service. The community was called upon to do many things. Hospitals all over the country were turning gay men away, so we had to channel our anger over this injustice to find a solution. In response, the community galvanized to create such organizations as the Gay Men's Health Crisis (GMHC), the world's first and leading provider of HIV/AIDS prevention, care, and advocacy.

Other men and women were mobilizing their anger in a different way, through direct-action, grassroots advocacy organizations like ACT UP (AIDS Coalition to Unleash Power). From the outside, ACT UP looked to be a manifestation of anger, fueled by rage and best remembered for bringing attention to the injustices of the AIDS epidemic. On the surface, the organization appeared to be a leaderless anarchist network, because their activities often involved disruptive civil disobedience. They were known to chain themselves together across bridges to stop traffic, forcing people to pay attention to their message. Other tactics were aimed at pharmaceutical companies or government agencies that had turned a blind eye to this disease that was killing thousands.

Yet even while their rage was boiling, at its center ACT UP had a laser sharp and brilliant strategic focus. Each and every act of passionate civil disobedience was undertaken for a reason, with a strategic goal in mind. Because people were dying every day, including many members of ACT UP, those heroic warriors simply didn't have the luxury of projecting anger for the sake of being angry. They understood keenly that in order to answer a higher calling, their moral obligation was to express their fury and rage to create change. And it worked. Regarding research funding for understanding the disease and developing effective treatments, access to clinical trials, and other key measures of progress in fighting the HIV/AIDS epidemic, the needle was in fact moved. Today, untold numbers of people continue to live because of these brave activists on the frontlines in the 1980s and 1990s.

Another way that the LGBT community galvanized during this time was through their involvement with the Human Rights Campaign (HRC). Formed in 1980 by Steve Endean, the organization existed solely as a progressive political action committee to build a donor base to influence elections and the legislative process. They called themselves the Human Rights Campaign, in part to reach a more expansive audience but also because frankly back then having an envelope in your mailbox from the Human Rights Campaign was less problematic than receiving an envelope that had the word "gay" on it. But make no mistake: the goal was to advocate for and protect gay, lesbian, bisexual, and transgender

Americans. Playwright Tennessee Williams wrote the organization's first fundraising letter in 1981. Today, HRC is the nation's largest LGBT advocacy organization. As the AIDS epidemic became a reality, HRC's first fight was to help elect members of Congress who would support decisions around funding and research to find a cure. For the next ten years, that is all the organization did.

After Dukakis lost his bid for the presidency, I left the Massachusetts State House and in 1990 went to work for Barney Frank, the first openly gay man in the U.S. House of Representatives. Even against the backdrop of AIDS, I was living the life I had imagined for myself during those dark days of high school. I left Congressman Frank's office in 1993 to work at the newly formed political action committee EMILY's List. My friend Mary Beth Cahill was the political director and she told me to pack up my car and come along. I didn't know much about the group, but it didn't take me long to realize that I had arrived at a very special place.

EMILY's List was started in 1985 by Ellen Malcolm and a group of women who had pushed for the Equal Rights Amendment and were leaders in the reproductive rights movement. Their mission is to raise money and elect pro-choice, Democratic women candidates to office. Their strategy was to financially support women early on in their political career by creating letter-writing campaigns and raising money nationally. It was a revolutionary idea at the time: the notion of raising small amounts of money from lots of women across the country. Because of the strength and commitment of the women involved, the amount of money these candidates were able to gather for their initial campaign filings more than often changed the dynamics of the race. Women with lots of early money were taken more seriously, becoming successful at raising even more money from the typical donors in their own home states and districts. Malcolm coined the phrase upon which the organization's name is based: "Early money is like yeast [EMILY]: it makes the dough rise."

My arrival at EMILY's List followed 1992's historic Year of the Woman, when more women had been elected to Congress than at any other time in history. The energy of that election cycle was fueled by the public outcry in support of Anita Hill, an African American law professor from Oklahoma. Hill had testified in opposition to Clarence Thomas before the Senate Judiciary Committee during his Supreme Court nominating hearing; she testified that Thomas, as her supervisor at the Equal Employment Opportunity Commission, had sexually harassed her. Many on the white male committee treated Hill with disrespect and hostility, enraging many American women, who turned out in record numbers later that year to vote for female candidates. These women channeled their disgust and anger into action, ensuring that in the future, Congress (and subsequently its committees) would be more representative of the electorate. Their success—and the ability to channel their rage into the electoral process—inspired me to think seriously about how I might be more effective as a change agent for the LGBT community.

In 2004, Elizabeth Birch, who had served as the legendary head of HRC for almost a decade, decided to leave the organization. She was replaced by Cheryl Jacques, a former state senator from Massachusetts. It soon became clear that Jacques wasn't a good fit for HRC. At the time I wasn't looking for a new job, but I found myself in the same Boston hotel as the HRC staff during the August 2004 Democratic National Convention. Elizabeth and her partner, Hilary Rosen, were sitting in the hotel lobby. I knew them through their involvement with EMILY's List. One of them asked, "How do you think things are going at HRC?" Never one to mince words, I told them exactly what I thought: Frankly, as an HRC supporter, I was angry. The LGBT community had just won the fight for marriage equality in the Massachusetts Supreme Court the year before. As a result, thirteen states had put constitutional bans on marriage equality on their ballots during the 2004 presidential election. HRC had put all its efforts and resources into the marriage fight in those thirteen states; consequently, the organization wasn't offering the community any additional paths toward achieving other forms of LGBT equality.

HRC had been the fastest, most impressive, social change organization in the country, but now it needed to communicate an agenda broader and more diversified than the battle in those thirteen states. I told Elizabeth as much. If we lost every one of those thirteen states, it would appear as if HRC had no other reason to exist. On Election Day in 2004 we did lose, and those losses became the measure of how the public judged HRC's effectiveness. In the aftermath of those elections, the LGBT community was actually blamed, even by some of our allies, for the Democrats' loss of the White House. Someone at HRC must have heard about my impromptu chat with Hilary and Elizabeth that day, because after the election I was called in to interview for the position of HRC president. I got the job.

It quickly became clear to me that the anger in the LGBT community was intense. There was just as much frustration directed toward HRC and the ineffectual leadership that had come before me as was projected at those we were supposed to be fighting. I had walked right into the middle of a complex, contentious scenario. At the time, LGBT issues were effectively the third rail of American politics. HRC had plenty of money, but we weren't spending it effectively to create change on the individual or societal level. As president, I had to address the community's anger, then figure out how to communicate a more diversified agenda. I wanted to present a more multidimensional, diverse portfolio of goals that, when achieved, we could measure as successes, so the whole ball game wasn't hung up on one important yet single issue: marriage equality. Our constituents needed to know that HRC was going to continue to fight for full marriage equality while also fighting for equality in every institution we could—the workplace, schools, hospitals, religious settings, and so on. Change anywhere would ignite greater change everywhere.

I also had to figure out how to present HRC to elected officials and politicians who had the potential to help us. They needed to see us putting our anger aside, to become a much more sophisticated ally. We needed a strategy that allowed us to advance our agenda with both our friends and our enemies. After the 2004 election, the White House as well as Congress was controlled by the Republican Party, whose leadership was unwilling to move any measure that would advance LGBT equality. In 2006 the Democrats took charge of the House and the Senate; we now had the opportunity to advance our long-sought-after legislative goals.

∷∷

During my eight-year-tenure with the Human Rights Campaign, I was able to take the organization from a deeply challenged body to a well-respected and effective political powerhouse. HRC oversaw the discriminatory Federal Marriage Amendment defeated in 2006 and the passage of marriage equality in eight states. Working alongside Judy and Dennis Shepard, we passed the Matthew Shepard and James Byrd Jr. Hate Crimes Prevention Act in 2009, after eleven long years of trial and effort. In 2010 we were able to repeal the discriminatory Don't Ask, Don't Tell policy. We achieved other smaller and lesser-known legislative and administrative victories that made significant change for LGBT people and their families. These successes were the result of a community-wide effort; together we channeled our collective passion over injustice, hatred, and violence to achieve the "impossible": full equality under federal law.

Other initiatives included launching HRC's Religion and Faith program to provide innovative resources for LGBT and supportive people of faith who want to stand up to those who use religion as a weapon of oppression. We created the All Children–All Families program for adoption and foster care agencies across the country. The Welcoming Schools initiative provides administrators, educators, and parents/ guardians with resources to create welcoming and respectful learning environments for all families. HRC's Healthcare Equality Index rates U.S. healthcare facilities on all policies and practices related to the LGBT community, including patient nondiscrimination, visitation, decision making, cultural competency training, and employment policies and benefits. Today HRC has more than one million members and supporters, including professional athletes, actors, television personalities, musicians, politicians, and countless straight allies.

Again, the successes of the Human Rights Campaign were not accidental. We implemented real tactical approaches to create social and legislative change, and I share these tactics throughout this book. Other movements for social change have not had nearly the impact and success HRC has enjoyed. Many such organizations now seek my guidance about the lessons I learned and the strategies I employed while at the helm of HRC. My success was the result of using incremental building blocks to motivate and cause palpable cultural change. These building blocks included channeling anger into action to achieve positive change; finding common ground with unlikely allies; making policy decisions based on shared humanity; knowing when to compromise and recognizing when you cannot give up; building coalitions; developing patience; and creating consensus. While these might not sound like radical concepts, when these sometimes counterintuitive ideas are implemented in specific and measurable ways, they can bring about profound societal change or minor personal changes, such as garnering a promotion. These processes have worked for me in the workplace, in my home life, and on the floor of the U.S. Senate. I know that these strategies can be equally effective for others.

1 CHANNELING ANGER INTO ACTION

These days the world seems to be an angrier place than it used to be. Let's face it: we're stretched in a million different directions, yet the world is getting smaller, more interconnected, and our relationships are rapidly changing. We used to compete against the business across the hall or across the country; now we must think about a global economy. Social media has provided a platform for anyone to express anything and everything they want and, democratically speaking, that's a good thing. Yet the sheer volume of it, the unfiltered nature of the content, and the anonymity available on these platforms create echo chambers for anger and hurtfulness to be exacerbated. This stress can generate an emotional reaction, and sometimes we choose anger over other emotions so that we don't appear vulnerable. We often use anger as a defense mechanism to get us through life's daily battles. As we're getting angrier, however, we can become less able to work together—to create social change or just to get along in the office. This anger can close us off from one another.

OUR ANGER PROBLEM

Anger, rage, fury—whatever you want to call it—is an emotion inherent in all people. Like other human emotions, we have the capacity for anger for good reason. Sometimes, it's okay to be furious. When you're confronted with a truly frustrating reality, the most useful thing you can do is to figure out how to use that anger: do you suppress it or find a way to use it to your advantage? Anger is something that you sense, that you legitimately and justifiably experience in the face of injustice and in moments when anger is called for. There are moments throughout U.S. history when righteous fury has been the source for creating positive, necessary, and strategic social change: Martin Luther King Jr. and the civil rights movement, Gloria Steinem and the fight for women's rights, the Stonewall riots and the struggle for LGBT equality. In all of these instances, constructive anger has been used as the fuel to build, not destroy.

The key is to understand in ourselves and in our communities when anger can be a productive resource or a destructive one. If you want to make change happen, use your anger as a gift, not a curse. Take the 2016 presidential election cycle, one filled with very different characters, from very different backgrounds, on opposite ends of the political spectrum who tapped into Americans' collective anger. They acknowledged it and fed it back to people in a way that served only to elevate and amplify the anger. The three prevailing voices in the 2016 presidential election cycle (that of Senator Bernie Sanders, real estate mogul Donald Trump, and former Secretary of State Hillary Clinton) addressed what each candidate perceived as voter anger. Throughout their campaigns, their messages reflected back the cause of Americans' anger, what each candidate believed voters were feeling.

Senator Sanders took the mantle of the Occupy movement and engaged voters with his message that a tiny wealthy minority has all the power, that the economy is rigged, that it's stacked against most Americans. He created a have-and-have-not dynamic, where his scapegoat was Wall Street, wealth, and high-income earners. Sanders gave validation to the have-nots for their anger at the haves. And while the anger and the sentiment he reflected was certainly warranted, he was never able to channel that rage toward a pragmatic or believable outcome. His own anger left doubts in the minds of too many voters about his ability to work as president in a collaborative way across party lines toward any solutions that had the possibility of becoming reality.

Donald Trump, on the other hand, did throughout his campaign what the United States has seen historically and politically in times of economic uncertainty. He tapped into the well of rage from America's working middle class, particularly white men who feel that life is unfair. Trump introduced something that is foreign to them (the "other"—in Trump's case, immigrants), something unknown that gives them someone to blame. He reflected a more dangerous point of view: *You're angry because life hasn't worked out the way you thought it would. The country doesn't look the way it used to. It's being overrun by immigrants who are taking your jobs, bringing the economy to its knees, and threatening your personal safety.*

Where Trump and Sanders are similar is that they recognized this well of anger throughout America; they mirrored something cathartic, a message that made people feel validated. In Trump's case, his message made them scared; in Sanders's case, it made them hopeful. Yet in both cases, the candidates' messages did not really do anything except regurgitate anger for the sake of anger.

The third point of view, which gets to the crux of this book, is that of Hillary Clinton—the only presidential candidate who channeled Americans' collective anger toward a realistic outcome. Throughout her campaign, she showed that she understands people are angry about injustice, but instead of reflecting that frustration back to Americans, she channeled the anger and used it to create a platform that provided people with a hopeful future. She gave them a sense of confidence that they can get to a better place. The outcome of the 2016 election will depend on whether voters are able to channel their anger and choose a candidate who works for them or are blinded by their anger and choose a candidate who works against them. The successful candidate is almost always one who is able to see that anger (passion) is a gift that can be channeled toward a greater good (creating positive change).

TURNING ANGER AROUND

Instead of shutting things down, however, anger can be used in another way. It can be the energy source that propels us to overcome systemic social injustice or the fuel that helps us to get what we want in a personal or professional situation. Processing anger and channeling it toward a positive outcome is a multistep process. The first step involves determining whether anger is even an appropriate response to something. If it is not valid, then you will learn what the appropriate sentiment, and course of action, should be. For example, if we demand that our legislative leaders take immediate action on an issue that is really important to us, but we hear that Congress won't be back in session for several weeks, that response—and that delay—is hardly a reason to burn down the buildings.

But if your anger is justified, the next step is to determine whether to express that anger and, ultimately, to what extent and how. When pressing for social change, you regularly meet resistance, which almost always results in justifiable anger. Your path forward depends on channeling that frustration and figuring out how to use it to get the outcome you want. In interpersonal relationships as well as in professional settings, there are many examples where anger is not a valid response. In these situations, it is best to consciously restrain your emotional reaction. Once you've stepped back a bit and taken anger out of the equation, and had an honest conversation with yourself and perhaps with your allies, you will realize that the decision you make about what to do with your passion will be the right one.

The key to navigating through anger and your initial emotional response to resistance or adversity is to be honest with yourself. If you can't do that, find people around you who can help. For instance, if you asked your boss for a raise, and she responded that she'd been meaning to talk with you about your poor performance, you might react to her criticism with defensive anger. You may feel that you and your boss are far apart in terms of evaluating your work. But who is right? If she is, then your anger toward her is misplaced. If you can't be honest with yourself and get past that anger, you're not going to chart a productive course forward. Sometimes trusted friends and coworkers can help you understand how you're viewed at work, so you can figure out how to move in a positive direction. However, if you find yourself in a situation where you've done the work and determined that your anger is justified, you still have to learn how to channel that frustration toward a positive outcome. Whether it's finding common ground, overcoming differences, or being able to listen strategically without the haze of anger filtering what you hear, we all have the potential to change any situation into a win. That's what this book is all about.

⁝⁝⁝⁝

On April 29, 2009, the U.S. House of Representatives passed the Matthew Shepard and James Byrd Jr. Hate Crimes Prevention Act (HCPA). The passing of the HCPA meant that thereafter the category of "hate crime" would cover not only crimes in which a victim's race, color, religion, or national origin were a factor but also those relating to a victim's actual or perceived gender, sexual orientation, gender identity, or disability. For the first time, gay and transgender individuals would have the same legal protections as everyone else.

In this case, protection for all came at someone else's tragic expense. Eleven years earlier, in 1998, two horrific hate crimes had been committed. Matthew Shepard, a young man living in Laramie, Wyoming, was tortured and killed simply because he was gay. James Byrd, an African American man, was singled out, tied to the back of a truck, and dragged to his death. I had the privilege of sitting in the congressional gallery alongside Judy Shepard, Matthew's mother, as the House of Representatives passed this landmark piece of legislation. She, along with her husband, Dennis Shepard, had spent the past ten years advocating, lobbying, and speaking out on behalf of this legislation that would give local law enforcement agencies throughout the country the tools they needed to more effectively investigate and prosecute hate-based crimes.

No one had been more courageous or committed to seeing this bill become law than Dennis and Judy. With their justifiable rage, through their grief, they saw that the perpetrators who had murdered their son went to jail for life. Then they took the next step and channeled their anger into action to create lasting social and legislative change. Judy wanted to ensure that no other American family would ever experience the pain and suffering hers had. They started the Matthew Shepard Foundation to replace hate with understanding, compassion, and acceptance. Working directly with the Human Rights Campaign, they toiled to get a federal hate crimes bill passed into law. The Shepards walked the halls of Congress for ten years trying to garner support and change the hearts and minds of legislators. Beginning in 2005, I stood with them. We worked together closely, and it was a true honor to be with Judy on the day we realized we had the votes to pass the bill through both the House and the Senate. President

Obama, who had worked alongside us for the bill's passage, was committed to sign it into law.

Before there can be a vote on any piece of legislation in either the House or the Senate, all sides (proponents and opponents) are given time to debate their various points of view. On that April day we sat through an entire morning of floor debate in the House. Although we had heard some misguided resistance to this bill over the years, most of the speeches that day were supportive. In their remarks many members of Congress paid tribute to Judy and her tireless work. I distinctly remember civil rights icon Congressman John Lewis commenting on Judy's steadfast dedication. Eventually Congresswoman Virginia Foxx of North Carolina chose to speak, in opposition of the bill. The fact that Matthew Shepard was murdered because he was gay, Foxx said, was simply a hoax. Everyone knew, she went on, that Matthew was the unfortunate victim of a robbery. Those of us seeking to pass hate crimes legislation, she explained, continued to perpetrate this hoax simply to gain support for the bill. She rambled on about how nothing that had been reported about the incident was actually true.

As I processed Foxx's hateful words, I was in complete shock. All of her claims were categorically false. I don't know if it was the adrenaline from the emotional roller coaster we all had been on leading up to this moment, but Foxx's comments enraged me like nothing had ever upset me before. Shaking, I turned to Judy. I thought we should put out a statement refuting Foxx's comments and get other members of Congress to immediately take to the floor and do the same thing. I was rising out of my seat with anger when Judy put her hand on mine. Quietly but firmly, she spoke: "This discussion isn't even happening. What's happening right now is that we are on our way, after eleven years, to winning. That's what is happening. Let's not let our anger or our emotions get in the way of our true goal. Our job is to see this bill through to victory."

Judy was right, of course. We had the votes we needed. Once the clock on the floor debates ran out, the bill would pass no matter what lies Virginia Foxx spewed. Our message in response would be to shine a light on the supporters of the bill. We would not give one more minute of airtime to the bigoted and misguided rhetoric of Virginia Foxx. She took her seat and was followed by Sheila Jackson Lee, a congresswoman from Houston and a civil rights pioneer. I expected that Congresswoman Lee would counter Foxx's argument, but she didn't even acknowledge it. Instead, she placed both Matthew and James Byrd as great civil rights pioneers in the tradition of Dr. Martin Luther King and Bayard Rustin. Like Judy, she channeled her anger over Foxx's vitriol into something positive. Her uplifting speech made all the people in the gallery forget about Foxx entirely. As we predicted, the bill passed in the House with a final vote of 249–175. The Senate went on to pass the bill in the fall, and on October 28, President Obama signed the HCPA into law. I was there. He commented to all of those attending that he had promised Judy and Dennis Shepard this day would come.

I recently spoke to Judy about our experience of getting HCPA passed. I thanked her for the lessons she taught me and told her how much I admired her grace during some very challenging moments. She reminded me that her grace and inner will didn't always come to her so easily. In the early days, just after Matthew's death, when she began visiting members of Congress and lobbying them, she was often overwhelmed and felt defeated by the intolerance and ignorance that some displayed when discussing hate crimes legislation. She wondered aloud to members of HRC's legislative staff whether she was cut out for the daunting task of garnering support for the bill. She often heard offensive and maddening comments. These conversations frequently brought out some of the worst vestiges of antigay sentiment. However, with the help of such brave allies in Congress as Senators Ted Kennedy of Massachusetts and Gordon Smith of Oregon, Judy was able to channel her anger into action. She never lost sight of her goal.

When we won and the bill was passed, Virginia Foxx's chief of staff called me. "Look, Joe," he said. "My boss wants to find a way to apologize to Judy Shepard. How can she reach her?" I called Judy and her response was clear. "To me, she doesn't exist," Judy explained. "Those statements don't exist. None of that exists. I will not be talking to Virginia Foxx. What will remain in people's memory is Sheila Jackson Lee's speech and President Obama's remarks as he signed the act into law. Those events are all that exist." I realized that Judy Shepard and Sheila Jackson Lee were wiser than me; they knew how to channel their anger and keep their eye on the bigger prize, the signing of the HCPA. While both women were smart and strategic, it didn't mean that they weren't filled with anger, even in that circumstance.

This was the moment when I understood that the emotion

of anger is a reality in all of our lives, and it has the potential to be a great gift. Anger was the primary emotion Judy had been carrying for over a decade, yet it had become a source of energy that kept her moving forward. For Congresswoman Lee, anger was like an adrenaline force, compelling her to be nimble and fast on her feet as she spoke so eloquently off the cuff. She never addressed Virginia Foxx; rather, she spoke above and around Foxx to get her point across. She channeled her fury toward attaining a positive outcome.

ANGER IS PART OF THE JOB

The ability to resolve conflicts and get what you want without causing ill feelings, disparaging others, or creating drama is the single most important trait for success in any workplace. It's an indicator of successful relationships, both professionally and personally. It's not enough to get your job done; it's how well you play with others that really counts. When we engage with others, there is the possibility that something they do or say will anger us. There are the small insults, the large transgressions, the feelings of being left out, or various emotional states of frustration, disappointment, and rage. In the heat of the moment, we tend to respond with hostility, blame, victimhood, or whining. These counterproductive reactions are unacceptable in the workplace because they are "conversation enders"—that is, they will not advance your argument or move the needle toward getting you what you really want.

A hostile reaction assumes that you're going to bring the offending person around to your way of thinking by hammering home your point. In other words, you are meeting anger with anger. This strategy is without merit in most situations. For example, if I were engaged in a formal debate, it is not out of the realm of possibility that I could win over my opponent to my way of thinking by providing well-researched facts. Yet heated discourse and argumentative conversation with a colleague or supervisor typically does not have that effect. In fact, there aren't many instances where an intense argument, whether it's about politics or cleaning up the break room after lunch, ends with somebody thoughtfully saying, "Wow, he directed so much anger at me that I completely concede the point. Joe is right."

In a formal debate some might strategically provoke their opponent, intentionally trying to anger them because an angry response is an unproductive response. When you're coming at someone with hostility, you're inadvertently putting them on the defensive, no matter how right you are. This strategy invariably entrenches an opposing faction into their position. In the best-case scenario the person you are attacking is calm enough to respond and explain their position. In the worst case, however, you have ratcheted up their anger. If this happens at work, you may possibly be fired. Either way, this strategy of provoking an opponent rarely works to your advantage.

Being wrongly accused of something is another situation where you may react with anger. You may try to resolve the accusation by placing the blame on someone else. Yet no one wants to hear anyone say, "That wasn't my fault." The truth is, when we think whatever bad thing happened wasn't our fault, there's a chance that it *might* have been. While there are real victims in the workplace of abuse or harassment, there is a possibility that you might have been at fault, or you might be viewing the situation in a completely wrong-headed way. If your natural reaction is to blame someone else—"I did my job; Joe didn't file the paperwork correctly" or "He hates me and I don't know why"—try to leave just the tiniest room for doubt. If your boss says, "I don't think you're committed to this job in the way you need to be," be open to the possibility that you may have in fact given that impression. It may not be true: perhaps you are committed to the job, and you may be very passionate about your work, but for one reason or another that passion isn't coming across in a way others see.

There may be instances where none of this is the case, where you actually have a sexist, bigoted boss, and you're the most brilliant person to walk through the door, yet she is going to bring you down. I'm not suggesting that every boss is always right. However, before you cry "victim," at least consider her point of view before you play the blame game. You need the maturity and the self-awareness to pause and ask yourself the question, *Does the possibility exist that I am contributing to the problem in some way?* Most often, the reality of the situation is typically somewhere in the middle.

Whining is a manifestation of blame. My friend Tom's wife is a classic un-self-aware whiner. Since I've known them, she has had three jobs and she is always working for "the worst boss." Nobody ever utilizes her talent, she complains. But she never pauses to stand in another person's shoes and ask,

"Do I *own* any of my problems?" A typical office whine is: "Management never thinks about including me in the conversation. They have a meeting and they bring lots of other people together, but my boss forgot to include me again." I can assure you, it is rarely the case that the boss achieved his or her higher level by not recognizing the extraordinary talent in the office. There are certainly times when some managers don't give young people the deference that they should. And it is important to bring young, diverse voices to the table. However, the invitation is usually extended to those whose views will add to the conversation, not to those who complained that they weren't included last time.

USING ANGER AS MOTIVATION

When things don't go our way, it's easy for someone to say, "Don't be angry." But, honestly, that isn't a realistic expectation. Few of us live completely Zen lives. More important, we *need* our anger to motivate us to take action, create change, and get more out of life. It's the discipline of putting our passion into action that helps us make the impossible possible.

When it comes to deeply interpersonal relationships, we are often counseled to not react with anger, but rather to be vulnerable and to express our hurt. This strategy might be effective in a relationship, where it's okay to say, "What you said hurt my feelings." However, it doesn't work in the office or when you set out to create sweeping systemic social change. Unlike personal relationships, where intimacy is achieved by being vulnerable, a professional, interpersonal dynamic is completely different. Office relationships are more transactional, the goal of which is for workers to demonstrate their value and in the process achieve self-satisfaction. The key to forming effective relationships at work is to stifle the instinct to respond with anger in a combative way and instead to find the most productive line of communication.

The instinct to react with anger can be difficult to overcome. But if you view every interaction with an eye toward getting what you want, using your anger productively can become one of the most powerful tools you have for creating enduring change. In Judy Shepard's case, for example, she used her fury positively to propel her cause. She was completely focused on the win and kept her eye on the prize. My immediate reaction was to lash out, but Judy used her rage as the energy source that powered her through *eleven* years of tireless lobbying. I imagine that every time something like the Virginia Foxx incident happened, Judy had a flash of anger. It's not that she had conditioned herself to no longer be upset, to no longer feel fury and despair about losing her son. Rather, she had the discipline to take the anger and put it somewhere else to be used constructively. Because she and all of us were ultimately able to keep calm and carry on, the hate crimes act victory was just the beginning of a new chapter in the fight for LGBT equality. This victory became the stepping-stone to HRC repealing Don't Ask, Don't Tell (DADT) and, ultimately, the Defense of Marriage Act (DOMA) and achieving full marriage equality for all Americans.

REPEALING DON'T ASK, DON'T TELL

When HRC stepped up its lobbying against the Don't Ask, Don't Tell policy following our hate crimes victory, it was the first time I heard utter indifference directed toward gays and lesbians from members of Congress. I saw how many members of Congress are motivated solely by what their constituents think (or what they *think* their constituents think). Already angry that LGBT people couldn't openly serve in the U.S. military, I became enraged at the indifference that some members of Congress showed about doing what I thought was so important. It was never easy for me to hear a representative say, "I don't care if gay men or women serve in the military; it's not my issue. I'm only concerned about keeping my seat in Congress, and what my constituents want." I didn't understand how they could be so unresponsive to such a key issue. I would have understood their position more if they had told me: "I have a very strong point of view about this, and I don't think that gay men and women should serve in the military." At least that was an opinion.

When I heard such a response, my instinct was to argue the point. I couldn't say, "What kind of an idiot are you?" That kind of conversation-ending hostility would get me nowhere. These congresspeople weren't interested in engaging on the issue, so I couldn't say, "Let me explain why it's important that gay people serve in the military." Putting my anger aside, I really listened to what they were expressing at the heart of their resistance. They were revealing that they just didn't care. HRC's legislative director, Allison Herwitt, kept reminding me: "You can't lose sight of what your job is. We're here to re-peal this awful policy." She taught me that we could build on small victories if we keep our eyes on the ultimate goal. With that in mind, I channeled my anger, took a deep breath, and focused on the long game.

"All I care about is what my constituents think," I heard over and over again from the legislators. "All I care about is doing the thing that is going to ensure that I don't lose my seat." I needed to better understand this apathetic response. Once I realized that it wasn't personal—it was about their constituents—we go to work. "Fine," the HRC team decided, "we'll go out to your district, your state, and we'll do the work of showing you that your constituents want you to vote with us—or, at the very least, that they don't care if you vote with us." From this, I learned that if you can win on the merits of the first interaction, every following interaction is likely to be a better, more effective one. This strategy transformed the way we lobbied. For example, even when I was angry about legislators' indifference, we could eventually get congressio-nal representatives to a "yes" vote. Instead of wasting time arguing around the merits, we would come to meetings with our polling numbers. "You need to vote this way," we'd ex-plain to an opponent, "because that's what your constituents want you to do."

Once the representatives saw the polls, they would often respond affirmatively: "I didn't care whether gay people serve in the military. But this meeting was a positive experience, getting to know you gay people, and working with very dif-ferent people that I never knew before. Maybe I'm open to the idea that gay people shouldn't be discriminated against at work either." These conversations changed their perspectives, and ultimately we garnered just enough votes to repeal the DADT legislation. Better still, at the next meeting, the same representative would tell me, "I voted with you and I'm stunned that my constituents didn't throw me out of office." These members of Congress were then emboldened to open the door to more positive change. They asked, "Okay, what's next on your agenda?"

WHEN ANGER IS EXPECTED

Sometimes the people you represent expect anger. The community is looking to their leaders who advocate on their behalf to validate their frustration. By validating it, leaders assure their constituents that their rage is understood and that they are taking the anger and using it toward advocating for change. This is why former President Bill Clinton was widely seen as such an empathetic leader. When he said to the American people, "I feel your pain," we believed him. We understood that he carried our collective pain with him. When people think an angry, forceful, combative pushback is warranted and you don't deliver it, you've let down your constituency. When I was the head of HRC, for example, I was often criticized for being less than passionate in the expression of my anger. There were many people in the LGBT movement who approached everything with a combative attitude, and there was all this pressure for me to demonstrate my anger in a specific way. Many wanted me to express the community's collective anger, but I chose to channel it into less hostile and more productive statements.

Yet there were other times when some suggested that my speeches came across as if I was too angry. Early in my HRC tenure, I was counseled: "Be careful of using too much angry rhetoric." Striking the right balance proved difficult. I tried moderating my tone and sounding less combative. This tactic worked in terms of finding more common ground with some in the LGBT community, but it left others feeling like there was no passion behind my words. I had to learn that different settings and situations demanded different messages. There would be many ways of reflecting back an audience's anger, but choosing the right tone to match the specific audience was a constant challenge. There are times when you can rail against injustice in a very public, cathartic way. This validates your feelings about your point of view, but may merely make you feel better in the short term; it usually doesn't have the effect of creating the lasting social or legislative change you seek.

In the LGBT rights movement at the time, some members of the community strongly believed that during every interaction, the opponent should feel our anger, and our only strategy should be to beat them on the actual merits of the point. The line of thinking was that if you fail nine times out of ten, but you win on one occasion, you've made real progress because you've changed one heart and one mind. However, I believed that we didn't have the luxury of time for that strategy—and I wasn't interested in losing the other nine votes. Some argued that my strategy was manipulative, the ugly business of getting the sausage made, because sometimes you're trying to get people who don't actually ever change their mind about LGBT rights to vote with you. I disagreed: we had to win any way we could. The victories were vital in the process of opening the door to creating a relationship with many of these members of Congress. Working this way allowed us to eventually change their hearts and minds.

I learned that simply saying that something has made you angry or offended really doesn't do much to change any situation. In fact, when someone says something that angers you, they often do so knowing full well what they are doing. To tell them that they've made you angry is not likely to get them to change their point of view. Instead, it is much more powerful to respond in these cases in a way that makes them understand that angering you was a mistake. Let them know that, rather than upsetting you, their anger has provided the energy and the drive you needed to win your point. In her testimony for the hate crimes legislation, for example, Congresswoman Sheila Jackson Lee used Virginia Foxx's anger to deflect the oncoming fury and to intensify her own message. Lee made her outrage felt loud and clear that day on the House floor. The strength and the power of her message—and the fact that she completely ignored her colleague's offensive remarks—in and of itself demonstrated just how furious Lee was. But the testimony sent her adversaries an equally important message: "You should think twice before you make those kinds of offensive statements again."

There were times when I was counseled to put my anger aside, be gracious, and just give thanks for something that I felt was a pretty low bar in terms of being deserving of my gratitude. These were the occasions where we would get something tiny. The LGBT community would say, "It's like we're begging for crumbs and we're thanking these people for not very much." For instance, at one point before same-sex marriage became legal, HRC was lobbying to eliminate the federal taxes that same-sex couples had to pay when they received domestic partner benefits. Married couples did not have to pay this unfair tax. A gay radio show host who was interviewing me at the time rolled his eyes when I discussed this tax. "Come on," he pressed, "what can that amount to? A few hundred dollars a year? It should be all or nothing. Forget about taking these crumbs they throw our way that then make them feel like they've done something big for us." Well, unlike this interviewer, I had met many men and women across the country who genuinely could not afford to pay that tax, who chose not to provide healthcare for their partners because of this tax. So while a strategy that led with anger and made clear we wouldn't take anything short of full equality may have felt good to hear on the radio, it did nothing to advocate for people whose economic circumstances were significantly worse than the interviewer's.

If the aim is to get something done, you have to measure the response that elicits the outcome you want against the response that might make you feel good in the short term (like getting angry) but isn't productive. The people who reach their goals are practiced at putting their rage aside and channeling their fury into smart, strategic, measured responses. The cost of leadership, as I learned through experience at the helm of the HRC, means never losing sight of the desired outcome even if it comes at a personal cost. Sometimes winning and the glory and gratitude that come with victory are mutually exclusive.

While working for social and legislative change, I didn't lose sight of my anger, nor did it diminish. Rather, I understood that if I could put the anger aside and meet my opponents where they lived, I would eventually bring them around to my way of thinking by removing the hurdles that existed for them. Channeling my frustration into a strategic plan— by demonstrating to members of Congress that the people who vote for them actually supported what we were working toward—enabled me to come back and fight another day. The positive experience of the first round actually opened their minds to think differently about the circumstances of LGBT people's lives. Next I outline two strategies that can improve the chances of that first round going well.

STRATEGY #1: BE PREPARED

Perhaps the first and most important step in channeling anger toward productive action is simply allowing for the passage of time. Don't react in the moment. Process what you're feeling, breathe deeply, and collect your thoughts. Your initial off-the-cuff response is almost never the most productive route toward a victorious outcome. To confront someone's position that you would like to change, or someone who says something that is so contrary to what you think is appropriate, requires a conscious act of actually pausing, acknowledging your natural emotional and frustrated response, and then identifying the more useful one. You might even have to write down how you really feel and throw out those notes, then clear your head and prepare to respond civilly.

For example, if you asked your boss for a raise or a promotion during your annual review, but your boss responded negatively, you'd be pissed. What if your boss told you: "I can't give you a raise because I think your attitude isn't what it should be. I don't believe you're as committed to the job as you could be." How could your view of your work and his perspective be so far apart? Understandably, your initial response would likely be an argumentative one driven by anger and shock. But if you instead pause after hearing this assessment, putting aside your anger and shock, you could find something to say that might salvage the situation. Take a measured, rational, intellectual evaluation of what your boss just said to you. Your response, more than anything else, needs to be one that acknowledges the boss's perspective. You could say, "Wow, this is news to me. We obviously have very different perspectives. Thank you for sharing this with me. I respect your opinion and am committed to getting this situation back on track so that we can be discussing a raise at some later point." This response demonstrates that you respect your boss's authority and that you are committed to participating in the solution. By responding productively, and less combatively, you've also acknowledged that there will likely be future conversations about a possible raise. You may be wondering, "What about the part where I stick up for myself or make the case that I think I do a great job?" All of that can happen, but only if and when your boss agrees that there is a path forward. When your position is more solid, when you are on a better path toward job security and ultimately a raise, you will be in a much better position to highlight what you have historically seen as your strengths.

If you know that you are going to be in a situation where something could provoke anger, prepare yourself ahead of time. For instance, when I was lobbying Congress with Judy Shepard for the hate crimes legislation, she accepted the strong likelihood that she would hear something that was going to enrage her. Going into a contentious scenario emotionally prepared may be half the battle. Prepare for the process of navigating the situation in a productive way. Expect the anger and prepare to put it aside. Then you can actually hear what is being said, work your way through the rhetoric, process what matters, and find inside yourself the appropriate and most useful response.

You might go into a situation where you are looking for several results, only some of which you'll be successful at achieving. For example, in meeting with your boss, if you ask for three things and he or she agrees with you on only one point, you'll be disappointed. The reasons your boss may give for not agreeing with your other two points will undoubtedly make you angry. But ask yourself, *If I wanted three things and I'm going to get one (as opposed to none), is that still a victory?* The answer is probably "yes." You lived through the ask to fight another day. You walked away with a positive outcome, which creates the opportunity to go back later and prove to your boss that you deserve the remainder of your requests.

STRATEGY #2: REPLAY WHAT YOU HEARD

The second strategy is put into play in the moment. You have to truly think about what's been said in a measured, thoughtful, intellectual way. Take a step back and figure out what's at the heart of what your opponent (boss, friend, or whomever) is saying. It might be hard to believe, but people had said to my face, "I'm okay with gay people serving in the military, but getting married? Never gonna happen." And this: "You want a raise? I think you're a deadbeat." Even when the vitriol is utterly offensive, try to put yourself in their shoes, then figure out a way to navigate a response that's going to create some movement toward getting what *you* want. What's at the heart of their disagreement? What do you know about this person? How have you prepared for the meeting? How can you continue the conversation? After all, the most unproductive thing you can do is to end the conversation.

As an advocate of LGBT rights, I carried the fate of many people on my shoulders, including many soldiers who wanted to serve in the military. That inspired me to not lose sight of the goal: I needed a vote count for repealing DADT. Keeping your eye on the desired outcome can be useful in all sorts of settings, particularly true in the workplace, when you have to evaluate your boss's opinion. Ask yourself, *Did I just get what I wanted, or did I get enough of what I wanted? Or did I get nothing of what I wanted? Did I go in looking for a raise but now feel like I'm going to get fired? How do I take that anger and channel it into something productive?* Discipline yourself to stand in the other person's shoes, to gain some sense of where they're coming from and what is at the heart of their opinion that contrasts yours. If you've asked your boss for a raise because you think you deserve one, and the response is, "You're not committed at all and your future here is uncertain," the truth probably lies somewhere in the middle.

You have to do the work to understand why your boss feels this way. The situation might have nothing to do with you: it may be that another employee is getting a raise and there's no room in the budget, or perhaps the company is having financial trouble. But with a greater level of understanding and a clear picture of your own strengths and weaknesses, you can stay in the conversation, not be combative, and eventually return to the discussion with your boss. One of my favorite rejoinders is, "This is the first I'm hearing of these concerns." This useful ploy brings the other person's guard down. By turning down the volume and having a more measured, thoughtful conversation, you might end up hearing something that gives you an accurate sense of what's really going on and gets you closer to getting what you want.

If you're going to successfully turn these circumstances around (or any other professional situation), you have to be open and honest about your own strengths and weaknesses. This involves strategic listening and overcoming sometimes long-held differences with others that you may not even realize you have. Once you can let go of the anger, you can create a measured, thoughtful, and detailed plan to get what you want. You're now ready to find common ground, which is the necessary first step to closing the gap between two disparate points of view.

2 FINDING COMMON GROUND

No matter where you're from or where you find yourself now, the circumstances of your life are largely dependent on your choices. However, they can be equally dependent on someone else. Your happiness with your partner is predicated not just on how much you love him or her, and how good you feel about yourself, but on your relationship with his or her family and friends. Your success at work is predicated not only on how you chart your path but also on how effective you are at getting a coworker to do something he doesn't want to but you need him to. This is a universal truth: the way you engage with others and how you construct these relationships is absolutely integral to getting what you want.

If there is one lesson I want you to come away with after reading this book, it's that you cannot underestimate the power of relationships. Thanks to our all-encompassing reliance on technology and social media platforms, the way we communicate with one another has fundamentally changed. The once bustling, noisy office environment is now a cone of silence. We are increasingly living in our own head, and when we do communicate with others, it's in less personal ways. For many of us, it's easy to get through a day without talking to anyone, at least not in person. Reading online news and posting comments on Facebook is not the same as having real conversations, especially when you have no idea who is reading your posts or tweets or whether anyone really even cares. For those who work in offices, even when the workspace is an open floor plan, there's often no noise: everyone is quietly working in their cubicles, getting whatever assignment or task done as quietly and efficiently as possible. We're silently responding to coworkers' requests or customers' questions by e-mail or text. Consequently, we're not developing connective relationships: we're merely providing answers.

To truly understand what's going on around you, you need to create relationships with people on a deep and meaningful level. The words that people deliver through e-mail or texting are only a part of what they are trying to convey. These communications often lack the sentiment and the emotion behind the words; understanding the emotional context is the key to strengthening relationships. Personal, one-on-one communication is *the* most effective way to develop a higher-level relationship. The strategy is to find one important thing that you have in common and then build on that shared interest. This is called *finding common ground*: identifying the shared humanity among people, no matter what their differences are. If there is any anger between you and the person with whom you are communicating, common ground is much more easily reached when you've put the anger aside.

Given today's rapid pace, the diverse and pressing challenges that compete for our attention, and the overwhelming amount of information that we are required to process on a daily basis, it's not surprising that anger and negativity come so easily for many of us. A sense of frustration or irritation seems to be the new normal. With that comes the tendency to think about how different we are rather than how much we are alike. Focusing only on these differences has the potential to fuel even more anger and frustration about the world. We are becoming poisoned by and addicted to the rush of anger, making social change nearly impossible. The most egregious example of this can be seen in the political gridlock of Washington, D.C.

The surprising truth, however, is that you can find common ground with people you never expected if you do not let your anger consume you. By setting your intention to slow down, act civilly, and look for the similarities instead of the differences, even when we are angry, we can automatically diffuse any inner hostility. If everyone would practice this ideal, we could create a more positive and productive environment. Even in an adversarial relationship, finding common ground allows you to create the space for deeper, more meaningful conversations. You are essentially saying, "We don't agree on the issue at hand, but in engaging with you at the level of what we both have in common, I am going to temporarily put our differences aside and open a line of communication to create a stronger relationship." If done effectively, this tactic helps the other person recognize mutual interests, which then forms the basis of a new, less adversarial relationship. Finding common ground allows you to reframe the way another person evaluates you, so there can be some amount of mutual respect, even if the differences are vast. Ultimately, you can use that respect and that changed perspective to create enduring change. Building common ground invites an intimacy into a shared humanity. It changes the dynamic of the conversation: by enabling you to put yourself in another person's shoes, you gain a better sense of what's in his or her heart.

THE POWER OF RELATIONSHIPS

I strongly believe that no matter what your goal is, you have to really know the men and women you are working with, whether they are your allies or your adversaries. To find common ground, start by being curious: listen to what others have to say and then ask questions. After that, when you want to get something done, you'll know what makes each of your colleagues tick. Use that knowledge to your advantage.

Refocusing relationships so they are defined by the hobbies, ideals, or principles that you have in common, as opposed to your differences, might seem somewhat obvious, but this isn't the way most people operate. In a lot of workplace settings, and even social situations, many of us define ourselves against others by the things that make us different: our heritage, schooling, gender, sexual orientation, or political beliefs, for example. We attempt to market ourselves as a special snow-flake, to show others how unique we are. In today's fast-paced, information-obsessed world, many people feel compelled to take what's inside and spit it out, to lead conversations with a snapshot of who we are and what makes us exceptional. Yet this reflex can be counterproductive and, worse still, difficult to undo. If you are constantly butting heads with someone at work, you might think about this person by defining how different their point of view is from your own. Those we don't agree with are always "the other"—that is, *You're either with me or against me.* With these preconceived biases about people, you might think, *He doesn't like my ideas, and he's old and outdated.* Or, *She doesn't even go to church.* Or, *I'm going to be able to work with him; he likes the Yankees!*

When I first started my career in LGBT advocacy in 2005, I found that highlighting differences was the most common way people engaged with one another in coalition, in activism, and in lobbying. Back then, my meetings began by acknowledging clearly stated differences. Whenever we went to speak with people who didn't necessarily agree with us, we immediately focused on how the two sides saw things starkly differently. These differences then became the subject of the conversation: the differences of opinion, the difference of life experience, the difference of subtleties within a legislative fight, the difference between whether someone was pro-gay or antigay. The HRC agenda was to try to change someone's position. My instinct, initially, was to say something like, "We want more equality in the workplace for LGBT people. We know you don't want to do it and that you don't agree with us, but here's why we think it's the right thing to do. As you might imagine, these conversations quickly became unproductive. This line of thinking was received as a nonstarter; focusing on differences didn't offer any space to reach a compromise. Asking for something vague like "more equality" wasn't directed enough to lead to any sort of change.

Instead, if you want something to happen, whether it's

small (like moving the photocopier) or huge (like creating a new workplace policy for parental leave for both men and women), I believe you have to begin with finding common ground. Rather than immediately going to the place where you are blinded by each other's differences, open yourself to the possibility that you and your adversary are more alike than you think. When you establish common ground, you'll find that people are more willing to work with you, to find compromise, even if they have opposing points of view. This creates a softer, more open-door atmosphere, which works best no matter the end goal because it highlights the similarities and puts aside the differences. This allows you to start the conversation from a place where you both agree.

THE ART OF FINDING COMMON GROUND

For some people, the work of finding common ground feels like engaging in meaningless small talk. But this chatter is much deeper than it looks. It's unlikely that I'm ever going to sway an anti-choice conservative Republican to becoming a pro-choice progressive Democrat, but over time I might soften up some of their views or open their mind to some ideas that they might not otherwise have taken into consideration. Imagine that you're at a dinner party, seated next to your diametric opposite on the political spectrum. You *could* let your time together be defined by those very significant differences. With that approach, however, the dinner conversation wouldn't go far because these attitudes are so emotionally charged. The evening would be a complete loss.

Or you could approach the evening by putting politics aside and trying to find some common ground. Discover what you and your dinner guest have in common by listening and asking questions until you find a shared interest. Then, even if you walk away from that dinner party without speaking about something substantive, it doesn't matter: you've made an ally, an authentic connection, out of someone with a different point of view. At the very least, you are a more enriched person for it. At best, the relationship might come in handy in some way you couldn't predict that night. When you first realize you're stuck next to someone so different from yourself, you might feel anger and frustration, which makes it hard to get to common ground. I am guilty of surreptitiously rearranging dinner place cards on more than one occasion. But as my friend Mary Beth often says, "It's a long life." You never know when that very person you thought you had nothing in common with could prove useful.

The first part of finding common ground is discovering and then acknowledging what, if anything, two parties collectively agree on before focusing on where they don't agree. In a business setting, common ground might turn out to be something two sides can work toward, even though it is not their top agenda item. For example, when I was working with Congress in 2005, we couldn't muster much support for marriage equality. We were fighting the Federal Marriage Amendment in Congress, which would have enshrined a ban against marriage equality into the Constitution. Issues like hate crime prevention and ending the ban on military service for gays and lesbians seemed more promising to tackle simply because there was common ground among members of Congress. It was an easier task to find common ground around the idea that no one should be the victim of hate-based violence, or that anyone who wants to serve his or her country should have the opportunity to do so.

President Barack Obama is one of the masters of the strategy of finding common ground. When he first made public his support for marriage equality, his language was specifically phrased so that it immediately established common ground with the American people who might not agree with him. During his interview with Robin Roberts of ABC News (excerpted below), every word, every sentence was purposeful.

> PRESIDENT OBAMA: As I've said, I've been going through an evolution on this issue. I've always been adamant that gay and lesbian Americans should be treated fairly and equally. . . . I've stood on the side of broader equality for the LGBT community. I had hesitated on gay marriage, in part because I thought civil unions would be sufficient . . . to give people hospital visitation rights and other elements that we take for granted. I was sensitive to the fact that for many people, the word "marriage" was something that evokes very powerful traditions, religious beliefs, and so forth.
>
> But I have to tell you that over the course of several years, as I talk to friends and family and neighbors, when I think about members of my own staff who are incredibly committed, in monogamous relationships, same-sex relationships, who are raising kids together, when I think about those soldiers or airmen or Marines or sailors who are out there fighting

on my behalf and yet, feel constrained, even now that Don't
Ask, Don't Tell is gone, because they're not able to commit
themselves in a marriage, . . . I've just concluded that for me
personally, it is important for me to go ahead and affirm that I
think same-sex couples should be able to get married.

Now I have to tell you that part of my hesitation on this has
also been I didn't want to nationalize the issue. There's a tendency when I weigh in to think suddenly it becomes political,
and it becomes polarized. And what you're seeing is, I think,
states working through this issue in fits and starts, all across
the country. Different communities are arriving at different
conclusions, at different times. I think that's a healthy process
and a healthy debate.

I think it's important to recognize that folks who feel very
strongly that marriage should be defined narrowly as between
a man and a woman; many of them are not coming at it from a
mean-spirited perspective. They're coming at it because they
care about families. And they have a different understanding,
in terms of what the word "marriage" should mean. And a
bunch of them are friends of mine, pastors and people who I
deeply respect.

ROBIN ROBERTS: Especially in the Black community.

PRESIDENT OBAMA: Absolutely.

ROBIN ROBERTS: And it's very a difficult conversation to have.

PRESIDENT OBAMA: Absolutely. But I think it's important for
me to say to them that as much as I respect them, as much as I
understand where they're coming from, when I meet gay and

lesbian couples, when I meet same-sex couples, and I see how caring they are, how much love they have in their hearts, show they're taking care of their kids, when I hear from them the pain they feel that somehow they are still considered less than full citizens when it comes to their legal rights, then for me, I think it just has tipped the scales in that direction.

One of the things that you see in a state like New York that ended up legalizing same-sex marriages was I thought they did a good job in engaging the religious community. Making it absolutely clear that what we're talking about are civil marriages and civil laws. That they're respectful of religious liberty, that churches and other faith institutions are still going to be able to make determinations about what their sacraments are; what they recognize. But from the perspective of the law and the perspective of the state I think it's important to say that in this country we've always been about fairness and treating everybody as equals. At least that's been our aspiration. I think that applies here as well.

Some of this is also generational. When I go to college campuses, sometimes I talk to college Republicans who think that I have terrible policies on the economy or on foreign policy, but are very clear that when it comes to same-sex equality or sexual orientation that they believe in equality. They're much more comfortable with it. Malia and Sasha, they've got friends whose parents are same-sex couples. There have been times where Michelle and I have been sitting around the dinner table and we've been talking about their friends and their parents, and it wouldn't dawn on them that somehow their friends' parents would be treated differently. It doesn't make sense to them. Frankly, that's the kind of thing that prompts a change of perspective; not wanting to somehow explain to your child why somebody should be treated differently, when it comes to the eyes of the law. If a soldier can fight for us, if a police officer can protect our neighborhoods, if a fire fighter is expected to go into a burning building to save our possessions or our kids, the notion that after they were done with that, that we'd say to them, "Oh but by the way, we're going to treat you differently. You may not be able to enjoy the ability of passing on what you have to your loved one, if you die." The notion that somehow if you get sick, your loved one might have trouble visiting you in a hospital. I think that as more and more folks think about it, they're going to say, "That's not who we are."

As I said, I want to emphasize that I've got a lot of friends on the other side of this issue. I'm sure they'll be calling me up and I respect them. I understand their perspective, in part because their impulse is the right one. Which is they want to preserve and strengthen families. . . . It's just that maybe they haven't had the experience that I have had in seeing same-sex couples, who are as committed, as monogamous, as responsible, as loving as any heterosexual couple that I know. And in some cases, more so.

If you look at the underlying values that we care so deeply about when we describe family, commitment, responsibility, looking after one another, teaching our kids to be responsible citizens and caring for one another, I actually think it's consistent with our best and in some cases our most conservative values, sort of the foundation of what made this country great.

I know you know we're both practicing Christians. Obviously, this position may be considered to put us at odds with the views of others. But when we think about our faith, the thing at root that we think about is not only Christ sacrificing himself on our behalf but it's also the golden rule. Treat others the way you'd want to be treated. I think that's what we try to impart to our kids, and that's what motivates me as president. I figure the more consistent I can be in being true to those precepts, the better I'll be as a dad and a husband, and hopefully the better I'll be as a president.

President Obama talked about his daughters coming home from school and referencing their friends who were the children of same-sex parents. He respected and acknowledged others who were resistant or finding their way on marriage equality. He did so not to in any way equivocate in his support, but rather so express: "See, you're like me on this journey. What happens in my household and in my church is happening in yours. If I got there, so can you."

FINDING COMMON GROUND WITH THE CHURCH OF JESUS CHRIST OF LATTER-DAY SAINTS

One of my most challenging experiences at HRC occurred in 2010, when I first met with the leaders of the Church of Jesus Christ of Latter-day Saints (LDS) in Salt Lake City, Utah. Our points of view could not have been more different. After all, in 2008 the Mormon Church had invested more money than any other religious organization in support of California's Proposition 8, which denied marriage equality to same-sex couples in California. Then, in 2010, Elder Boyd K. Packer, president of the Mormon Church's Quorum of Twelve Apostles, announced to Mormons around the world in a radio address (which was also placed online) that same-sex attraction was "impure and unnatural," changeable, and he characterized same-sex marriage as immoral. This kind of language from Packer was not only unpleasant, it was dangerous. His words infuriated me; they could have tragic consequences. Suicide was on the rise in the LGBT community, often set off because of bullying. In Utah, the home base for the LDS Church, the number of homeless youth that identified as LGBT was over 40 percent.

Bruce Bastian, a former Mormon who lived in Utah and one of the most generous supporters of HRC, counseled that we needed to act decisively. We needed to approach the church with a clear understanding of their vulnerabilities, in a way that would get them to pay attention to their divisive and dangerous language. We knew that the LDS Church leadership hated bad publicity, and they had had a public relations crisis since Proposition 8. In response to Packer's address, HRC created an online petition for individuals of any faith to sign. The statement, directed to the LDS Church, read: "You can say what you want and you can do what you want, but when you do something that causes a young person to feel like they should take their own life, or run away from home, it's shameful."

The petition got 150,000 signatures. We printed out every page and planned to take them in boxes to the Mormon

Temple in Salt Lake City. My colleague Sharon Groves, HRC's Religion and Faith program director, came with me. Before we arrived, church officials called to express this sentiment: "We understand you're coming. We understand you're bringing news crews. We understand you're bringing boxes of petitions. Here's how this is going to work. Go to this corner, stand here, somebody will come out, somebody will take them." The meeting did some good. We showed the LDS Church that we were paying attention, and we reminded the LGBT community in Utah and throughout the country that we understood the deep challenges many faced within their own faith groups.

We were more surprised by our follow-up meeting with LDS leaders. Jim Debakis, a longtime, well-respected Salt Lake City activist, was part of a small group that had been meeting with LDS leaders. I was in Salt Lake City for a fund-raiser and talked with Jim about setting up a meeting for him, Bruce Bastian, HRC communications director Fred Sainz, Sharon Groves, and me. Some members of the LGBT community felt that we shouldn't further engage with the LDS Church, because they viewed it as enemy number one. Yet Bruce convinced me that the meeting had the potential to be productive, that getting the right people around the table held the possibility for a more significant outcome. I agreed to the meeting. I knew that we needed to find some common ground, some thread that we could hang the whole conversation on in order to make some progress.

Having heard about some of the private, clandestine conversations that had been happening between local LGBT activists and LDS Church leaders, Sharon was prepared for a different kind of conversation and sought common ground. She asked the church leaders if they could maintain the tenets that guide their faith but understand that HRC's mission involves trying to keep young people from killing themselves. She looked for common ground around family. "We know Mormons love their kids," she said. "Our hope is that you can see that young people killing themselves or leaving home and often ending up on the streets is not something any of us want." It was a long way from, "We're trying to get gay people married." Instead, Sharon created a place where it could be possible to find some common ground. Their response was in fact very positive. The church leaders responded with respect for the work of HRC. They too did not want young people to end their lives. The LDS elders ended up deleting that offensive language from the text, which was then circulated around the world.

Our minimal understanding of the LDS community as those Christians with the funny handshake and bizarre underwear was transformed into a more thoughtful, less arrogant understanding of a faith that has been and continues to be meaningful for millions. Their understanding of the LGBT community as angry, aggressive, sex-obsessed, amoral people became more complicated after our meeting. They were forced to see HRC's authentic commitment to youth who were hurting. This encounter helped HRC's religious work hereafter to include a strategy of engagement with those who think differently than us. This initial conversation was the beginning of great changes within the LDS Church.

Today, the Church's position is vastly different than it was just five years ago. They are not patently antigay in their rhetoric anymore. They no longer aggressively demonstrate against marriage equality, and they have taken steps to speak out against discrimination of gay people in the workplace. Many of its members still hold the same old antigay views; they just don't speak about or act on these beliefs in the destructive ways they did in the past. They have a much better understanding of the harm that overt homophobic language causes young people.

Since those days, there have been further changes in the LDS Church. In the 2012 battle for marriage equality in four states, the LDS Church was surprisingly quiet—a far cry from their noise in 2008! Recently they publicly supported a non-discrimination act in Utah stating that a gay person should not be fired because of his or her sexuality. The Church also created a gay Mormon website that, while far from perfect, does not demonize LGBT people in the ways it had before. These positions are far from ideal. The Church continues to make unfortunate mistakes, such as the 2015 decision to disallow the Mormon children of same-sex couples to be baptized until they are eighteen (a blunder that surprised even many in church leadership and resulted in fifteen hundred Mormons leaving the LDS Church). But unlike the days of Proposition 8, after *this* unfortunate decision, church leaders immediately qualified their position and talked directly with the LGBT community.

The model of overcoming anger and finding common ground is hard work, and it doesn't result in instant transformation, but it is the most powerful strategy, particularly in religious contexts, for making lasting change. I imagine that a time will come when the LDS leadership will change its position and view LGBT people as children of God. I believe that our deep, if difficult, engagement and search for common ground will have helped pave the way.

WHEN THE ENEMY WANTS TO BE YOUR ALLY

It is nearly impossible to grow—socially, emotionally, intellectually—or to enact lasting social change unless we open ourselves up to finding common ground, no matter how divergent our views might appear. After the LGBT community lost Proposition 8 in California in 2008, which meant that voters supported a constitutional ban on same-sex marriage, I was invited to appear on the *Dr. Phil Show* as part of a panel to discuss the issue. There were three pro–marriage equality and three anti–marriage equality people on the panel, and the audience was split in terms of support. I sat with the mayor of San Francisco, Gavin Newsom, and civil rights attorney Gloria Allred. The other side was represented by Maggie Gallagher, a leader in the fight against marriage equality; evangelical religious leader Jim Garlow, the minister of one of the biggest churches in southern California; as well as chair of the Proposition 8 campaign.

Typically I try to find common ground when I debate someone on television or the radio. I find that it brings their guard down a little bit and makes them like me a little more than they initially intended. While my adversary might start a conversation disagreeing with me on ten different points, before the conversation ends, I might eventually bring them around to seeing my way of thinking on four of those points (that might be as much of a victory as I will ever get). However, on this show I couldn't get a word in: Gloria Allred, not surprisingly, did most of the talking, and the mayor and I sat there quietly, watching the circus unfold. I knew it would be uncomfortable, but I never expected how vicious the show would become. Some audience members yelled, "You're going to hell, and you're never getting married." The panelists seemed to validate the audience's collective emotions. Where could we go with that? It was like a bad episode of *The Jerry Springer Show*.

When the taping ended, there was so much anger coming from both camps in the audience that security guards had to come in and empty the theater; the panelists were shown to the green rooms. Somehow, in the craziness, Gavin Newsom and Gloria Allred went in one direction, and I was stuck with the opposition. Much to my surprise, though, while we were waiting to be released, Jim Garlow tried to engage me in a conversation, even after he had laid out on national television exactly how I was going to spend my afterlife. "If I'm ever in Washington," he asked me, "can I come see you?" I was speechless, slightly offended, and sort of confused by the request, but I pulled myself together. "Sure," I said. I was certain I would never hear from him again.

A month later, Reverend Garlow called me. "I think it's important for us to learn more about one another," he said.

I recognized his agenda right away: he was searching for common ground. One of the first things we talked about was that my father had died when I was young. We had this interesting conversation not about being raised by a single mom but about having a parent die young. About a month after this conversation, Garlow was interviewed in *Newsweek*. "I'm going to say something that people will be surprised by," he said, "but I consider Joe Solmonese to be my friend. In a handful of personal conversations with him, I have a greater understanding of the circumstances of his life and a greater respect for who he is as a person and whether he thinks this or not, I think of him as a friend."

Garlow went out of his way to get to know me and to put our politics aside. Even though we were still very far apart ideologically, he had done the work to find common ground. The more information I gave him, the more I humanized myself. It wasn't much, but it inspired him to identify me as a friend. This may not ultimately change his heart or mind, but it will make it impossible for him to see me as a caricature of a gay activist. As someone with influence in the world, Garlow holds a lot of power with his pronouncements. If nothing else, his opposition might become more thoughtful and nuanced because he has a relationship with someone on the other side. This subtle, more thoughtful change could make a huge difference to an LGBT person who follows Garlow's pronouncements. If they see that Joe Solmonese is his friend, it may help them to see that their own lives could hold value even in the most nonaffirming spaces.

IDENTIFYING ALLIES THROUGH FINDING
COMMON GROUND

A big part of the strategy for the fight for LGBT equality was to put ourselves under the umbrella of the civil rights movement. We took it upon ourselves to describe our fight as a modern-day civil rights struggle. We understood that using the language and the imagery of the civil rights fight was good for us. It seemed obvious to me that our movement was so clearly the country's current civil rights struggle. And it seemed to me that African Americans should recognize and sympathize with the discrimination we faced and should be among our strongest supporters. Yet while some brave leaders like Coretta Scott King and Julian Bond were supportive, the sentiment among many in that movement was decidedly different. They believed that our experiences of oppression and discrimination could not be (and should not be) compared to anything African Americans experienced and that we had not earned the right to coopt the language and imagery of their civil rights struggle.

I felt strongly that we needed to do a better job of finding common ground with the current leadership of the African American civil rights movement. In 2008, on the heels of our defeat with Proposition 8, I had the opportunity to meet with Reverend Eric Lee, a heroic civil rights activist and member of the Southern Christian Leadership Conference who was living in Los Angeles, and Wade Henderson, a personal hero of mine and the head of the Leadership Conference on Civil Rights. Both men asked me the same questions: What had the

LGBT community done to help illustrate for African Americans that there were life experiences and issues that we had in common? What had we done to illustrate to African Americans that their enemies were our enemies? What role had any of us played in remediating their issues—either historically or today? In other words, these great leaders were asking me if I could identify the common humanity among the people we needed more than they needed us.

With this understanding, thereafter I tried to work more in conjunction with the African American civil rights community to speak out around issues that were important to them. HRC continued to strike common ground in terms of how we worked together. We reminded people that while we respected the differences in oppression that our respective communities had faced, we were grateful to take the lessons learned by pioneering civil rights activists and to work alongside them in forging our own fight. Once the civil rights leaders knew they could count on us, that became our common ground.

FINDING COMMON GROUND AS MARKETING

One of the turning points in the fight for marriage equality came when we began to realize that we had to make some significant changes in the way we looked for common ground with the larger American public. Among the many things we did, we ran a variety of focus groups to determine what would be the best way to reach common ground. Our initial tactic had been to advertise our efforts as "we LGBT people are just like you, and we should have the same things that you have."

That effort espoused that the LGBT community looks just like everyone else, with homes, cars, kids, and jobs. The message was that we're successful and we contribute to society, that we're your neighbors and coworkers and you're probably lucky to know us, to work by our side, and to have us living on your block.

However, that strategy didn't work. It turned out that most Americans just didn't see the inequities we faced with the absence of marriage. We were, perhaps, the victims of our own success when it came to integrating into mainstream society. The response we got during focus groups was, "You guys don't have it so bad. Why do you want marriage anyway?" We didn't just have a problem with those who were opposed; we also had a complacency problem with those in the middle. So we switched gears to find a different kind of common ground. Instead of saying we were just like everyone else, we refocused our message: "If you and your spouse *couldn't* be married, here are all the vulnerabilities you would face. Think about your overall welfare and healthcare and the financial decisions you make about one another and your children." Same-sex couples who want to marry are victims of that inequity, the new message was. We often told the story of two eighty-five-year-old veterans who met during World War II. "Look at these men. They are Americans heroes. After forty years together, if and when one of them dies, the other will lose his home and half his pension because they weren't able to marry." The emotion behind such stories, and the understanding of real tangible loss and vulnerability in the absence of marriage, moved people beyond whatever resistance they had harbored. This basic message became our fight for common ground.

CONVERSATION STARTERS

The truth is, common ground doesn't have to be profound: it can be a shared interest in finding the best pizza in town. I once found myself at a bar watching an NCAA basketball game during March Madness. I was meeting up with a colleague who was bringing along his friend who we thought could be a valuable connection. We found common ground instantly talking about the Boston Red Sox. This was beyond ironic because I know nothing about the Red Sox even though I'm from Boston, but the one thing I *did* know about was then center fielder Jacoby Ellsbury, because my mother was a big fan, and I had once seen him in a restaurant with my friends Mary and Becky, who were huge fans. We ended up talking about the Red Sox all night. I couldn't chat about the game or the season or even the strengths or weaknesses of particular players—I knew nothing—but I could talk about the institution and the way so many Bostonians felt about the team. I could tell it was a different kind of Red Sox conversation for him, but I could also tell that we had bonded. I'd never guessed that we'd found common ground around our hometown sports team.

To get started, take a quick audit of yourself. Ask, *How curious am I? How easy is it for me to pull something from nothing? How much work do I have to put into the appearance of being curious, and how observant am I? How easy is it sitting, looking at somebody? If I had to engage in a conversation, and start asking you questions right now, how easy would it be for me to do it?* Curiosity doesn't come naturally for some people, but you can enhance yours just by taking time to be present in your own world. Then work on conversation starters where you can find a shared interest. With strangers, start at the most micro level: what people are wearing, reading, eating, drinking, and so on. If you know who you are meeting with, prepare ahead of time by Googling them and discovering a few facts. Just a few starters will help you find common ground.

MAKING NEW CONNECTIONS AND LISTENING

Consider making a connection with everyone you meet, no matter how different they may seem compared to you. Throughout most of my career, whether I was working on campaigns or leading the biggest LGBT organization in America, my office was always filled with people just like me. I was the liberal, leftie, pro-choice, pro-gay Democrat. My entire work life, 100 percent of the people I worked with, also fit that description. But when Ted Gavin and I started our business, for the first time I found myself working with some people whose ideology and political affiliation were very different from mine. Today I even work with a handful of Republicans.

When a new guy comes to the office who looks different from you, has a nasty temperament, seems to hate his job, or is bringing his anger toward his lot in life into the workplace, don't just take a step back and dismiss him. We are all more than what we initially appear to be. Take the initiative to find common ground. The shared humanity you discover may be very narrowly focused: a sliver of an interest that helps him give you the respect you need, and you to give him the respect he needs, to be able to work productively together. That is all you're going to accomplish, but that's success. Someday, because you've stayed at it, for example, this guy will become your ally. Making new connections, although initially uncomfortable or unnatural for you, is a complicated and important exercise to go through to strengthen the working relationship with the new person or even with someone you've known for a long time, such as your mother-in-law.

⁝ ⁝ ⁝ ⁝

One of the greatest ways to find common ground to get things done, including changing someone else's position, is to be a good listener. Instead of talking, taking what's inside of you and spitting it out, start listening so that in the long run you can be a more meaningful contributor to the conversation. In chapter 3 you'll learn that how well you listen has everything to do with how quickly you can find common ground. The temptation to shut down relationships or conversations with those who anger you is a bad strategy for achieving change. My advice is to always be strategic rather than outraged. The next chapter explores how to be a better listener when someone else is talking. This allows you to form a strategy that takes into account all the information available to you, which enables to you get what you want.

3 LISTENING MINDFULLY

If I've learned one thing in my advocacy career, it's that you'll get farther if you are a good listener rather than a good talker. "Listening well" doesn't mean you have an uncanny sense of hearing, or that you can understand a foreign language or two. It refers to being actively aware during a conversation so that you can intellectually process what the other person is saying. Good listeners take in information rather than spitting information out and understand that the process of receiving information ultimately serves them when they need to present strategically useful information at the right place and time. Effective listeners are always the most curious individuals. Being a naturally curious person means that you have a much easier time asking questions and that you are genuinely interested in the answers you are receiving. Unharnessed, angry, off-the-cuff responses, on the other hand, negatively impact your willingness to listen and greatly diminish your curiosity. Without channeling your initial anger (which might be a very legitimate, valid response), you can become deaf to other people's thoughts and ideas that may in fact benefit you.

Regardless of your political affiliation, many people characterize former President Bill Clinton as one of our smartest presidents, while former President George W. Bush is often satirized for not being particularly intelligent. One of the reasons for this is that anyone who knows or has spent time around Bill Clinton will tell you that he is the most curious person they've ever met. He is curious about everyone he meets and about abstract, distant, and obscure ideas and fields of study. His ability to take in massive amounts of information makes him a truly unique individual. In the case of George W. Bush, I don't think you get to be leader of the free world by being dumb. However, this former president left me with the impression that there was little that he was innately curious about.

When you are curious and ask questions, you give other people the sense that you are interested in them. People respond to that. They want to be thought of as someone other people think are worth spending time with. For example, if you are on a date and ask lots of questions, the other person spends most of the time talking about themselves. If you asked them how they would rate the date, most likely they will say they felt like it was interesting—and that you were interesting. The fact that you didn't talk much but asked questions and let them talk about themselves creates bonding and connection. I am a curious person. I ask lots of questions based on what I am observing, whether I'm at a friend's house or a business dinner. I create conversation triggers that could be about almost anything—from someone's appearance, to what they say or do, to the surrounding environment. These triggers allow me to quickly find common ground, so that I can move the conversation along to a productive place.

One challenge I have in my professional life, now that I am no longer with the Human Rights Campaign, is that I work with mostly straight men whose interest in sports far exceeds my own. Even though I'm a curious person, and lately I'm trying to pay more attention to sports, I'm never going to be able to compete with any guy when he's talking about a particular player or a specific game. I try to take the conversation to a peripheral place where we can find common ground, but this isn't easy. I'm always grateful to the person who makes the effort to do this with me. My colleague Stan Mastil, for example, is an avid sports fan. He is also somebody that people enjoy being around and want to work with because he tries to be inclusive and he's a good listener. Stan goes to great lengths to talk about sports with me, either one-on-one or in a group setting, especially about high-profile gay athletes. In 2014, when the NFL teams were choosing their draft picks, Stan said, "Hey Joe, if defensive end Michael Sam doesn't get picked, don't think that it is an antigay sentiment within the NFL. He's just a little bit too short and a little bit too slow." I didn't know who Michael Sam was. "I don't understand anything that you're saying," I admitted.

Stan made a great effort to explain to me the football terminology as well as Michael Sam's pros and cons. He was thoughtful enough to engage me in a place he thought I would be curious about within his own range of interests. He was genuinely authentic. Even if you're not interested in what someone's position or passion is, you can always find a way to bring their interests into the conversation. Stan made the tactical effort by asking himself, *This is an office full of people whose common ground is sports. But this interest doesn't apply to Joe, who's someone I should find some common ground with. Here's how I can bring Joe into the conversation and bring him into the group.* It's generally an effective communication strategy.

BE ACTIVELY CURIOUS

One of the inherent perks of being both curious and a good listener is that people will notice you. Being a curious listener makes you a more interesting, empathetic employee, friend, or partner. These traits are vitally important in the business setting, where so much of the work is collaborative. How teams come together, and whether or not you are included, has as much to do with how well you work with others as with your actual skill set. Even if you think, *I am the best person for this team. I'm the smartest person. I'm the best accountant. I'm the best programmer,* most people will prefer the *second* best person if they just like working with that employee. Even if you are not the fastest at whatever it is that you do, if you can make others feel that you are listening to what they say and are willing to take what you hear into account regarding the work, you'll be the employee others choose to collaborate with.

One of the first things I learned when I was working on political campaigns was how to conduct myself at a fundraiser or dinner party. I was taught that whenever you walk into a social setting, bring your curiosity with you by coming prepared with five questions that you can ask anyone. My questions tend to be harmless, universal, and designed to elicit information and keep the conversation going. My opening question is typically, "How is your family?" whether I know that person's family or not. This question shows that you are interested in someone on a personal level. It's also very useful if you can't remember if someone is married, divorced, has kids, and so on. People will answer the question as it applies to them. For instance, I asked this question once to a man at a work conference. I assumed that he would answer by talking about his wife, although I wasn't entirely certain that he was married. Instead, he spoke at great length about his father's terminal illness. I was able to talk about the recent loss of my mother. Each of his answers was a prompt for what my next question would be. Eventually we got around to business, but that part of the conversation was completely on his terms, and I was ready for when he moved the conversation in that direction.

One way to become more curious is to be a more informed person. Carve out twenty minutes to half-an-hour a day to read the newspaper (online or paper copy) and get caught up locally and globally. Familiarize yourself with four or five different subject areas aside from the front page, depending on your interests. It could be sports, arts, food, real estate, movies—whatever. Before you know it, you are going to find things that are of even greater interest to you. I read the *New York Times* from cover to cover every day. No matter where you are in the world or in the country, the *New York Times* is the national newspaper of record. Its many sections are devoted to diverse and interesting subject matter. The *New York Times* may not be your ideological stripe, so you can read the

Wall Street Journal. Both papers are national publications with many different areas of focus, with nationally recognized writers with nationally recognized reputations. If you are really pressed for time, just read the "Week in Review" section on Sundays, where journalists process and analyze the news through a particular filter. With this prep, you'll have ample conversation starters at the ready. When I was writing this book, for example, everyone in New York or Washington, D.C., where I spend a lot of time, was talking about the sold-out Broadway hit *Hamilton.* Because I read the *New York Times* every day, even though I couldn't get tickets, I could still strike up a conversation about the show.

Another way to be more curious is to try to learn ahead of time as much as you can about the people you're going to be talking to. Before a meeting, I learn all I can about a person. Almost no one is beyond a Google search. If you know you're going into a negotiation, or will be asking for something, knowing about the person puts you in a position of power. I don't meet with anyone new (personally or professionally) without running their name through Google, Facebook, and LinkedIn. Reading about them always gives me a different perspective. I might find a new piece of information that might help me find common ground with the person at the meeting.

One caveat: Be careful about how you throw around the information you find online. You want to be knowledgeable, but you don't want to appear as if you've been stalking the person. You don't want to say something like, "Hey, congratulations! I understand you just had your twentieth anniversary. We have a mutual friend on Facebook, and I found my way over to your side." My friend Dani once was going for a new job and looked up her potential new boss's political giving. She decided to reference this data in her interview, introducing the politician's name and party affiliation into the conversation. Unfortunately, her strategy backfired. The new boss couldn't stand that politician and had been forced to make the donation because that person had supported his industry.

MASTERING THE ART OF MINDFULNESS

The best listeners are those who have mastered the art of mindfulness: being fully in the present moment and participating in whatever is in front of them. Mindfulness allows you to look at all angles of a problem and solve it because you are present to every aspect of it. You are able to approach a situation from a more neutral point of view, where you are in effect creating the space necessary for change.

I consider myself to be a mindful listener because of my inherent curious nature, the fact that my parents raised me to be a well-mannered person, and the reality that I actually listen to (and do not interrupt) people when they talk. In fairness, though, I grew up in a world where information came more slowly, and it was conveyed in a limited number of ways. We had network news, radio, and print newspapers and magazines. We live in a very different world today. Because of the overwhelming availability of data everywhere, all the time, young people in particular tend to have the greatest challenge simply sitting and listening. Millennials (those born between

1982 and 1994), understandably, are more dismissive or suspect about outdated modes of ingesting information. Yet it's in their best interest to put information in its proper place, and mindfully listening is ultimately still one of the most powerful tools of communication.

Sitting quietly and listening to someone talk for fifteen minutes is no longer the standard way to receive information. Today we can get information in an exponentially larger number of ways: texting, emailing, the Internet, thousands of television channels, and so on. The sorting and processing of this overabundance of information has to happen much more quickly, therefore we have much less bandwidth to deal with external dramas. Not everyone is going to get you information in fewer than 140 characters. In face-to-face interactions, especially for millennials, it might seem like people talk incessantly. Yet we all have to learn how to listen when they do. Even if you think that it is the most antiquated way of conveying information, actual conversation should always be reserved for the most important interactions. How well you listen and process that medium says everything about how effective you are going to be at responding or executing the instructions given.

Mindful listening can be challenging because it is a passive activity: you are at the whim of the person you are listening to. Although listening begins as a passive activity, as you get better, you'll see that it is actually an active exercise. It's like the research phase of writing a paper or doing good detective work. You're downloading all the information someone wants to give you. Then you end up controlling the conversation, without being overbearing, because you've let them express everything they think. At this point, you can choose how to respond and move the conversation in the direction you want to go. I actually saw a great example of this on an episode of the Bravo television series *The Real Housewives of New York*. It was the sage Bethenny Frankel who said to another woman: "Your problem is you always come in hot, like a missile." The implication was that her friend always came into a conversation loaded with what it was *she* wanted to talk about, without creating the necessary space for any feedback or a meaningful exchange.

While *The Real Housewives* may not be the best place to draw philosophical examples about manners and how we engage with one another, I find myself using the phrase "coming in hot" more than I ever thought I would. Most people, especially those new to the workforce, have a tendency to come into any conversation hot, invariably saying: "Listen to me. This is what I want to talk about. This is what I want you to do for me. This is what I need." However, if you combine listening, learning, asking questions, and soliciting information, you'll be able to hear what it is that they say and then formulate your response to move them closer to your goals.

"THE ASK"

When I worked for EMILY's List, I truly believed (and still do) that ensuring that the face of Congress look like the face of America was important and worth funding. But if I went into a fundraiser "hot" and started talking about what excited

me about the organization, I was often not successful at raising money. Founder Ellen Malcolm came up with a counter-
strategy to this approach. She realized that the key to being
an effective fundraiser, or to be better at any job, was to be a
better listener.

To get what you want—whether it's money, a promotion,
or an answer to a question—mindful listening allows you
to take control of the conversation, by keeping the person
you're speaking with engaged. During any meeting, you need
to listen to what the other person has to say and consciously
take the information in, and *then* move the conversation by
asking questions that build on what you've just heard. You can
process their responses as you formulate your own, each time
getting a little bit closer to getting what you want. At EMILY's
List we would teach campaign fundraisers how to be better
listeners at a seminar we called "The Elements of an Ask."
The process involved starting a conversation by first asking
questions to give you a sense of the person's mind-set. Based
on the information learned, you formulate a specific ask and
then hold back from saying one more word until you receive
a clear response.

Sometimes the excuses people gave for not donating
money made me a little angry. For example, if a potential
donor told me they hated politics, had no interest in elections
or the people running in them, I would think to myself, *How
can this woman not care about something that has such an impact
on her life and the lives of people much less fortunate?* But I would
need to put that anger aside in the moment and instead craft
a response that would move these people toward their wallet.

So I would acknowledge what they had just said, by repeating their statement, then I would immediately move to finding common ground, a place where we could agree. "I hear that you hate politics," I would say, "but can you tell me what the public policy implications are that would most adversely impact you?" By getting that donor to articulate her opinion, we would get to common ground.

Once I changed my strategy to lead with questions (instead of "coming in hot"), even if I was meeting with a group I had struck out with before, I brought in more donations. When people feel that their feedback is part of a solution, they are more engaged donors. For instance, if they cared deeply about the issues that EMILY's List candidates championed, or felt empowered by simply seeing more women in office, I would steer the conversation not toward the electoral "process" but rather toward the "outcome" or the result of the "process." This redirection usually worked to put donors and fundraisers in a place where it was appropriate to make a financial ask.

WINNING THE REPEAL OF DADT BY LISTENING

Mindful listening has dozens of applications throughout my typical day. It can be your most effective secret weapon during any conversation between people with opposing views. Sometimes during a negotiation you feel affinity toward one another; at other times, you are negotiating with an enemy. In this case, the anger you inevitably feel can cloud your thinking. The key to successfully negotiating anything is to bring the conversation as close to a civil transaction as possible, which is more akin to the process you would go through with someone you actually like. When you find yourself in a position in which you must negotiate, understanding where the resistance to your point lies is the key to getting what you want. If you are negotiating a business deal, or trying to buy a house, you don't go into the meeting and state your demands: "I deserve a raise!" Or "I shouldn't have to spend more than $50,000 over market value." Instead, if you set the ground-work by creating an ongoing conversation, soliciting from your adversary information that will tell you what he or she feels are the strengths and weaknesses of your argument, then you can improve your offer to match expectations.

The journey toward repealing Don't Ask, Don't Tell offers up the best examples of the importance of mindful listening because, like many legislative efforts to expand rights for peo-ple, it involved a highly emotional and passionate group—in this case, gay and lesbian soldiers who were serving heroically yet silently. It was often terribly frustrating and disheartening for them to sit in coalition meetings and listen to conversations with elected officials about poll numbers, election results, and political expediency. To them, and to me, this issue was such a no-brainer: it should be a conversation about basic fairness and anyone's right to serve. The difficult yet important work of listening reminds us that just because we think everyone should agree with us doesn't necessarily mean that they do or they will. While we might not like what we hear from people in response to asking for what we want, we have an obligation to respond to what we hear and not what we *want* to hear.

I talked to people across the country about their views on

the Don't Ask, Don't Tell policy. Taking the time and energy to listen to their positions, rather than telling them about my views, I was able to understand what was at the heart of their opposition to repealing this law. Then I was able to share my philosophy from a clear and centered place where the opposition could hear my argument and respond appropriately. More often than not, I was able to move the needle forward and get what I wanted out of the conversation. If I had approached each congressional representative and shared my point of view, I would be less likely to get an honest response. I couldn't say what was really on my mind, which was: "I'm here to talk to you about repealing Don't Ask, Don't Tell, which I'm sure you agree is a discriminatory piece of legislation, so it's important that you support our efforts to repeal it."

Instead, I started the conversation by asking, "How do you feel about the Don't Ask, Don't Tell policy?" By doing so, I wasn't leading or characterizing the conversation. If the response was, "I don't really care about Don't Ask, Don't Tell; I'm not that interested in it unless my constituents tell me they are," then I would have to respect the outcome. That response was at the very least an honest one, which allowed me to move the conversation to address my next point. As troubling as it may sound, this was the response I got from many members of congress. Oftentimes, my conversation with congressmen about the importance of gay people being able to serve in the military would just end at this point. But I couldn't let my emotions and my anger cloud my listening and ask, "What kind of an idiot are you?" Not the productive thing to do. Instead, I would continue to ask questions rather than make statements, in a way that allowed the legislators to speak their truth in a nonthreatening way. Through mindful listening, I would endeavor to really hear their truth.

If my goal was to get a specific member of Congress to vote with us, I would respond with facts: "A vote's coming up, and you're going to have to vote yes or no. I'm interested to hear what it might be that would get you to vote yes for repealing DADT." In one case, I spoke with an elected official who was supposed to be a leader and an agent of change, but he told me that all he really cared about is not being out of step with his constituents. I had to meet him where he was. I knew what we had to do next. We visited that congressman's district to demonstrate to him that the people who vote for him in fact want him to repeal DADT. Ultimately, this was the key to getting him to vote yes.

Another response I received from members of Congress went along these lines: "I don't think gay people should be able to serve in the military, because I think it's bad for morale if you make straight men and gay men have to take a shower together." While such statements made my blood boil, I had to respond in a way that would, at the very least, keep the conversation going and, at best, lead to a vote to repeal the law. The work that we did to change that Congressman's mind was not the work I had always pictured myself doing, but it demonstrated that we listened. Our strategic response was a result of what he had to say, not what we had to say. The difference represents a subtle but significant behavioral shift. Even though we knew that we were on the right side of history, we had to adopt the mind-set of the person we were listening to and use *their* reality as the springboard to get to yes.

For instance, some members of Congress—and leaders in the military—felt that it was important to do an implementation study and fully examine how the repeal of Don't Ask, Don't Tell would influence military readiness and morale. At HRC, we felt that this was not only unnecessary but an insult to the men and women who were currently serving honorably. However, we listened to our allies, who counseled us that the study was something that had to happen. It would give political cover as the document these folks could point to when they finally agreed to vote in favor of repeal. And in fact, most of the members of Congress who told us they needed to see that study completed ultimately voted for repeal of DADT.

The strategy of adopting the opponent's mind-set and using *their* reality as the springboard to get to yes works when you are trying to change minds on an individual basis. However, moving groupthink is an entirely different story. The way that the American people were moved on the subject of Don't Ask, Don't Tell happened just how you would expect: brave men and women who had been serving in silence came out and shared their stories—over and over again. They put a face and a name on a conflict, selflessly showing what it means to be heroic. The small role I played was simply getting Congress to catch up to where I believed the American public already were on the issue.

DISRUPTING CHRONIC INTERRUPTING

One of the easiest ways to be a better listener is simply to stop talking. When I watch most people engaged in a conversation, it seems that they're right on the edge of their seat, biding their time until they can jump in and talk again. The minute they find a tiny, little opening in the narrative, they jump in with what they want to say. A classic example of this is when people try to finish one another's sentences. Yet when they do, the other person often tells them: "Well, no, that's not what I was going to say." If you're a lot more invested in speaking to hear yourself talk, you are going to turn off the people who need to listen to your ask. I used to work with a guy named Rob who, like many people, talked much more than he listened. He talked to sound smart, and he talked because he was insecure about what people thought he knew and didn't know. This was Rob's undoing. Whenever a group of people were pulled together to solve a problem, nobody ever wanted him around. Nobody wanted to listen to him.

Don't be Rob. A mindful listener is a patient listener. By waiting to respond, you can pick up on how the other person's message changes as they rattle on, then use that shift in the message to your advantage. It's likely that you may have a different opinion than you would have had if you had started speaking two-thirds of the way through what the other person was saying, rather than waiting until they finished. What might happen is that the substance of what you want to say doesn't change, but the content changes because of what you heard at the end of their statement. This is the difference between the learned discipline of "I won't speak until you are done, which will allow you to say something that may inform my argument" instead of "I am going to say what I want, regardless, so that I can get what I want." These are two different motivations.

Let's use an example from my office during a formal performance review with a young employee named Samantha. She wasn't making herself part of the team. I wasn't impressed with her work, and she wasn't getting along well with the rest of the staff. When I asked Samantha why she was having problems in the office, she responded with a laundry list of complaints about how she felt underappreciated by the staff. She paused briefly, but because I was quietly listening and watching her, it seemed to me like there was more she wanted to say. The last thing Samantha said, almost as a postscript to the conversation, revealed all: "I don't know. I'm also upset because my father died last Thursday, and I'm still feeling upset." I had no idea that this major event had happened. Now that I knew, I could completely understand how Samantha's personal life was affecting her work. Because I let her finish speaking, and really paid attention—sensing she had more to say and giving her the space to say it before jumping in—she gave me a piece of information that would largely reform the tone and substance of my response. I couldn't brush the problems she was having at work under the rug, but I could change the way I delivered my message. "I am really sorry about the loss of your father," I said. "Please let me know if there is anything I can do to help. Let's see if we can constructively separate what's going on with you personally from what's going on in the office. And maybe we need to give the healing process a bit more time."

An even better strategy for active listening is one I learned from working with reporters. More than anyone I know, these men and women are specifically trained to be good listeners. They understand the longer they don't say anything after they ask a question, the more a subject is likely to talk; and the more the other person says, the more information revealed. Many people have a tendency to jump in and fill the silence in a conversation to stop it from becoming awkward. Reporters know this and so will often ask completely open-ended questions and then wait until there is a prolonged silence before they ask the next question. Over the phone this can be a little disconcerting because you don't have visual cues that the conversation is continuing, yet this technique is still effective. For example, a reporter will call me up and ask a question; I will answer and then there is silence. "Are you still there?" I sometimes ask. The reporter will respond: "I am still here." That very brief moment of silence may very well be a clue that you're on the line with an expert listener.

GETTING PAST ANGER WITH CURIOSITY AND MINDFUL LISTENING

In 2007, HRC hosted a live televised debate on Logo TV with the Democratic presidential candidates who were there specifically to address LGBT issues. The moderating panel included *Washington Post* columnist Jonathan Capehart, singer

Melissa Etheridge, and me. Going into the debate, none of the Democratic candidates except Congressman Dennis Kucinich of Ohio supported marriage equality. Many activists were angry that none of the frontrunners supported marriage equality. There was a sense in the community that some of the candidates personally supported it, but felt that for political reasons they couldn't be public with their support. There was a lot of pressure on me from leaders in the LGBT community to use my time to advocate for marriage equality. Every minute of every day leading up to the debate, someone wanted to know how I was going to fill my five minutes with Senators Barack Obama, John Edwards, and Hillary Clinton.

I decided that in each of those conversations I was going to use my time to express my curiosity. I was going to ask each candidate what was at the heart of their resistance to marriage equality. My question would be, "Why do you not support marriage? What's at the heart of your resistance?" Getting that answer would be much more productive to moving these people toward marriage equality than me talking at them as an advocate or delivering a message on behalf of the LGBT community. I thought that if I could hear what was at the heart of their resistance, it would better arm us, as a movement, with what we needed to do more broadly to try to change their minds.

During the event, I asked my question, then sat back and listened. Each of the senators offered a different answer. I knew that on a number of previous occasions, John Edwards had offered that it was his faith that kept him from supporting full marriage equality. When it came time to interview him, I asked specifically what it was about his faith that would cause him to be opposed to the civil institution of marriage, for which we fought. Immediately, Edwards said that he was wrong to use his faith as an excuse, essentially admitting that it was both wrong and damaging to our cause to conflate the civil institution of marriage with the religious sacrament of marriage. As an elected official it would be wrong to do that. From there, however, he wandered off and came back to simply restating all of the things he was for, such as the repeal of Don't Ask, Don't Tell. Our brief time together certainly didn't move him in the direction of supporting marriage equality, but it confirmed for me that he probably did support marriage personally, but felt that it would be too politically dangerous to do so. It confirmed that taking him at face value and confronting him with alternative faith-based arguments would have been unproductive.

The reason for Edwards's resistance, while flawed in my view, was quite different from the resistance Senators Obama and Clinton offered. Both of them essentially dodged the question, answering with various reasons why it was a matter best left up to the states. In Obama's case, at the time that was as far as he was willing to go. Clinton explained that the state-by-state process was one that would introduce marriage equality to the country in a more sustainable way. Their answers—or nonanswers—led me to believe that both of them probably supported marriage equality on a personal level, but that in the context of the election it was a politically unsustainable position to take. But because we asked and listened and tried to learn more about what was at the heart of their resistance, we walked away from that experience better armed to move them in our direction.

APPEARING MORE MINDFUL

When I'm speaking with young people, sometimes there's a look on their faces, or body language, that tells me they're not listening. They have listened to everything they're going to hear and moved on to the formulation of a response. They're shaking their heads, like, "Yup, yup, yup." They've listened to the first couple of sentences, jumped to a conclusion about where the conversation was headed, and started to formulate a response before I've stopped talking. While it is certainly important to be processing information you're receiving and formulating a response—as we discussed earlier—you can't do it if you've essentially stopped listening to the other person after the first sentence. The body language I'm talking about looks like this: there's a forward movement with their body, and every time I take a breath, they lean forward, ready to start talking. In one example, my business partner Ted and I were doing a review with one of our younger employees. He seemed to be processing what we were saying in short-hand: "Okay. Got it." Ted said to him, halfway through the conversation, "You're making me uncomfortable. Your body language and the look on your face are making me want to get through what I'm saying to you faster than I am saying it. You're so eager to want to start talking." We've all experienced this. Having someone look at us while we're talking in a way that says, "Okay, wrap it up, I'm ready to go."

In today's rapid-fire world of information overload, slowing down to really take in information is easier said than done. It's an exercise that takes practice, especially for millennials.

It means understanding that you're playing the long game. You won't be the most talkative person in the meeting or at the dinner party, but you'll probably have the best ideas when it comes to solving problems as well as the most meaningful friendships. While you may not be the life of the party, you'll be a trusted confidant, someone people want to continue to connect with long after the party's over. Being mindful and present can be tough. This is particularly true when you're dealing with someone who talks a great deal. You've gotten the point and you've moved on. Check yourself and bring your focus back to the conversation, away from trying to remember what time yoga class starts or what you need to pick up at the grocery store on the way home. Redirect the conversation in a polite way when there's a natural break, but be present enough in the conversation to know whether you've cut them off or simply helped them move forward.

In one way or another, I spend a lot of time counseling the people around me to be good listeners. Sometimes I encourage them to simply slow down and be more accurate in choosing their words; other times I persuade them to consider another person's point of view in a more respectful way. Pay close attention to the feedback that you get from friends and coworkers, and try to determine if they are telling you to be a better listener.

:: :: :: ::

Once you've established common ground, and really heard what your adversary wants, then you can explore why there is resistance to your goal. Unfortunately, most people are naturally conflict-adverse, so it's not always easy to get at the heart of someone's resistance. I've found that when you take the time to establish common ground and listen to what people have to say, however, it makes the work that much easier.

4 OVERCOMING DIFFERENCES

If you want to strengthen the working relationship with a colleague or bring somebody around to your way of thinking, you have to sort out where the similarities and differences are in your positions. Once you're completely clear about your differences, you can better understand why the other person holds the position they do. Far too often, we set out to change someone's mind without truly understanding *why* they believe what they do. As you can imagine, you'll figure this out much more quickly if you've put your frustration aside and done the work to find common ground.

Any disagreement can elicit a range of negative emotions—from mild annoyance to moderate irritation or full-blown fury. There are cases when there is no emotion at all, and you'll find common ground in a completely dispassionate way. More often than not, however, a disagreement will elicit some degree of emotion because all of us feel inherently strongly about our own point of view. You have to work out this emotion to make a clear-headed decision on what you should do. That doesn't mean that you're not entitled to be angry or annoyed: you just need to use that frustration as the gift it is to energize and clarify your position, especially if you need to stand your ground.

If a coworker won't participate in your project, for example, and you're annoyed that you have to do all the work yourself, you may have an easier time finding out why they won't work with you once you've calmly approached them and established common ground. Then you can figure out the stumbling block, or where the difference of opinion lies: is the problem the way he or she feels about the project, or does the colleague have a problem with you in a leadership role? Once you have a better working relationship, you'll have the ability to ask straight out: "Is it me, or is it the project?" Whatever the response, you have to work with what you've been told. For instance, if the problem is the project, perhaps there is a project of a lesser scope that you two can work on.

There are two types of differences that can be negotiated. The first are personal, ideological differences. The second type of obstacle is cultural, which we will discuss in a later section. Working in the LGBT movement, I constantly came across people whose views were best described as antigay. Their cringe-worthy perspectives obviously made me angry, but I worked hard at making sure that our early interactions were filled with efforts to find common ground. Then I took on the task of understanding these differences. The more I worked at it, the more I was able to gain a better grasp on their resistance. Eventually I could make sense of what motivated their views, odious as they were to me. For some opponents, their antigay views were rooted in fear—fear of change or of a lifestyle they didn't understand. For others, there was an innate sense that they might actually be gay, and their antigay views were simply a deflection. Understanding these very different motivations would lead me down very different paths in terms of how we would overcome our differences. Comprehending what was at the heart of our disparities—particularly if I felt like their views were based in their own fear or misunderstanding—often helped to ease my anger.

Starbucks CEO Howard Schultz clearly understands the complex gift of anger and how to anticipate it and then channel it productively for social change. Before the state of Washington legalized same-sex marriage, he spoke out publicly in favor of marriage equality. He did so with a clear understanding that he would need to find common ground and overcome differences, with the state's citizens as well as his shareholders. When Schultz made his case, he always reminded people that the country was a diverse patchwork of relationships and that recognition for same-sex couples depended on where you lived. For him, the argument was simple: a lack of relationship parity from state to state was a problem for a mobile workforce and a problem for his company. As a corporate leader in Washington State, it was important for Schultz to be able to attract and recruit the best and the brightest people to work at Starbucks. If he attempted to hire a marketing person from Boston—only to be turned down because that man was married in Massachusetts, but would no longer be considered married in Seattle, this discrepancy created a bottom-line problem. So while Schultz's messaging may have been a bit "wonky" and grounded in what was best for Starbucks's bottom line, he brought people to his way of thinking by showing them a way around their differences. Even if you didn't support marriage equality, you would be hard-pressed not to understand and respect what was at the heart of Schultz's motivation. His statements ultimately had an enormous impact on the fight for marriage equality throughout the entire nation.

OVERCOMING DIFFERENCES AT THE INSTITUTIONAL LEVEL

The second type of obstacle to be negotiated is often cultural—that is, the way an organization or institution views the people that comprise it. During my time at the Human Rights Campaign, beginning in 2005, I knew that while it was important to change the makeup of Congress, it would take some time—maybe years. Until both the House and the Senate were occupied by pro-LGBT majorities, we wouldn't have much success advancing a legislative agenda. However, we still had to figure out a way to get what we wanted. We knew that the ultimate goal was to pass laws in Congress to protect all people from workplace discrimination. In order to do that, we had to create a systematic way for corporate America to change its view about their LGBT employees and to change their willingness to do something for us.

My predecessor at HRC, Elizabeth Birch, began the work of appealing directly to corporations, hospitals, schools, and religious institutions to try to change the experience in these settings for LGBT people. This organizing principle became one of the most significant catalysts for change in the LGBT movement. The goal was to create a more equitable, welcoming, and inclusive experience. For instance, within the American workplace we understood that it would be some time until we could get laws passed that would prohibit workplace discrimination against LGBT people. Instead, we went directly to corporate America and talked with them about implementing policies that would do just that. When we began working with corporations, there were eleven million people in Fortune 500 companies. Even though our long view was that we had to change all of America in terms of the perspective on discrimination in the workplace, we started with these eleven million. We were able to claim significant victories for this segment of America.

We started by finding common ground. The one thing we knew corporate America wanted was a more productive and satisfied workforce. HRC's argument was that in addition to LGBT people seeking workplace equality, we also wanted the opportunity to bring our whole authentic selves to work every day, and in doing so, to excel and truly contribute as sustained and empowered employees. After establishing that common ground with corporate America, HRC worked on closing the gap between what LGBT people needed for enhanced workplace equality and what each individual institution was prepared to give. Before each meeting, we identified what could be the obstacle that would keep us from getting what we wanted. Then, each ask—from inclusive nondiscrimination policies to domestic partner benefits—was justified in a way that benefitted not only LGBT people but all of the stakeholders. We made the case again and again that anything the companies or institutions did to foster a more welcoming and inclusive environment was simply good for the bottom line. With each "yes" we received, the differences grew smaller as we worked together to create a more vibrant workforce and to tap into a powerful consumer base.

We faced the challenge head-on. We didn't beat around the bush. We were open and honest about what we wanted for the LGBT community, knowing that the answer might be "no." And we faced plenty of obstacles. Initially, I don't want to say more people said "no" than "yes," but many people thought what we had to say was important and interesting—they just couldn't figure out how to implement at the workplace. Imagine the sheer amount of bureaucratic work among corporate America of redrafting untold workplace policies. For HRC, a policy that included LGBT people in an internal nondiscrimination policy was a straightforward ask and the right thing to do. However, many corporate human resource departments had all sorts of questions about the implications of such a move. As the years went on and our asks of companies continued, so did the process of overcoming many of these same hurdles. HRC's most recent ask of our corporate allies was to cover the costs for an individual who had made the decision to transition from one gender to another. It has taken *years* to implement these polices throughout corporate America, but many companies have worked with their legal departments, human resources, and insurance providers because they have been committed to finding a way to foster the best environment for diversity and inclusion within their companies.

We just kept pounding away with a single message: that what we proposed was in corporate America's best interest, that our ask was always grounded in what was best for their business. As companies adopted each new benefit or workplace policy, it had multiple effects. They of course communicated the policy information to LGBT workers, but on a deeper and more profound level, these new policies said to LGBT employees: "You're important, you're safe. You matter here and we encourage you to bring your whole self to work every day." Today, most companies have employee resource groups that represent various workplace constituencies like LGBT workers, working moms, communities of color, and others. They network, advocate, and ensure that the interests of their various constituencies are being met. The brave and trailblazing members of LGBT employee resource groups were vital to HRC's success (and remain so today) as we began working with companies.

Although this strategy seems rather straightforward and obvious today, it wasn't when HRC first started advocating for antidiscrimination policies. Grassroots activists would often say that my language in talking about what we wanted from corporate America was tempered and watered down. They couldn't understand why I wouldn't just demand justice at work for LGBT people and frame the argument in simply "doing what's right." The truth is, at the heart of the resistance for many in corporate America wasn't a lack of understanding what was "right" or just. It turned out that "doing what's best for the bottom line" was a much more compelling promise—one we knew we could deliver on.

Eventually HRC's work with corporate America developed into a rating system called the Corporate Equality Index. We began rating companies on their LGBT workplace policies and issued an annual report. Within a few short years, it became critically important for many companies to score a perfect 100 percent, year after year, on the index. And LGBT consumers began using the index to make spending decisions. Today, such companies as American Airlines, Marriott Hotels, and so many others proudly advertise their 100 percent rating when marketing to LGBT consumers. What's more, LGBT consumers and their multibillion-dollar spending potential have motivated many more companies to excel on the Corporate Equality Index. I see a clear link between HRC's early work in corporate settings and the ability for LGBT people today to more fully integrate into the fabric of American society. We replicated the work we did with corporations in hospitals, schools, and even religious institutions. The plan was to have civil conversations with different types of institutional leaders that could actually create tangible protections for LGBT individuals.

In healthcare settings we found common ground by agreeing that all people walking into a doctor's office or an emergency room should have equal access to healthcare and be treated with dignity. Our goal was to work with hospitals to send a clear message to their admitting staff, nurses, and doctors about the policies they were going to implement to create a more welcoming environment for LGBT people and same-sex couples. Yet there were obviously some stark disagreements with healthcare workers about how to do this. Laws like the Health Insurance Portability and Accountability Act (HIPAA) limited healthcare decision making to next of kin or spouses. In the absence of marriage equality for same-sex couples, LGBT people were unable to participate in—or even be in the same room with—those we recognized as our spouses. But healthcare providers were bound by the law, so in some cases we were at an impasse. However, we were able to move forward by convincing hospitals to include LGBT people in their patients' bill of rights. HRC worked with hospital administrations to increase the number of people allowed in a hospital room beyond what they defined as "immediate family." We respected their commitment to follow the laws—regardless of whether we agreed with them—and the hospitals gained a greater empathy for the lives LGBT couples and families had built.

In addition to the hospitals, we went to colleges and universities, asking what they could do to create a more welcoming and inclusive experience for their LGBT students. In more progressive parts of the country, there is good work being done by schools with LGBT student groups, but in other regions, and on more conservative campuses, there remains much work to do, whether it's a college campus dealing with issues around violence and sexual assault against women or issues involving LGBT students or students of color. Because students are constantly rotating through school and there is complete turnover every four years or so, HRC tried to create a sense of permanent change on campuses by working with administrators and alumni. We supported the efforts of such groundbreaking groups as Athlete Ally, founded by Hudson Taylor, which works with college athletes and athletic department to end bullying and homophobia in sports.

OVERCOMING DIFFERENCES IN FAITH

Age, race, political affiliation, upbringing, and life experiences can cause sharp differences of opinion with friends or co-workers. Our individual religious beliefs and faith traditions can be the most formative—and sometimes the most difficult to get past. As someone who does not subscribe to a particular faith tradition, I have found that the divide between myself and those of deep faith can be a deep one.

Of all the institutional settings HRC approached about making lasting change for the LGBT community, the religious institutions seemed to be the most daunting. Ask anyone where the greatest obstacles exist in the advancement of LGBT equality and they will likely tell you that religious doctrine and, in many cases, the words of religious leaders, have been our greatest deterrent. All too often, we see those with a deep religious faith portrayed in the media as anti-LGBT, and LGBT people portrayed as those who live separately from religious communities. This is simply not true. For this reason, the Human Rights Campaign launched a Religion and Faith program in 2005. Harry Knox, who sat on the President's Advisory Council for the Office of Faith-based and Neighborhood Partnerships, started the program. HRC's Religion and Faith program continues to provide innovative resources for LGBT and supportive people of faith who want to stand up to those who use religion as a weapon of oppression.

The Religion and Faith program initially set out to do many things—most of them with the long view of change in mind. We understood that often the only voices people heard on

TV or in the press were religious leaders speaking out against LGBT equality. Yet we knew that there were many religious leaders who supported our cause. We needed these leaders to speak up, so we gave them the resources and the training they needed to do the work on our behalf. We created an incredibly vital multifaith advisory committee. We gave them media training, sent them across the country to speak and debate, and booked them on television whenever possible. Eventually, when you turned on the television and saw a debate about LGBT equality, it was often between two religious leaders— one with a viewpoint against us and the other speaking out on behalf of the LGBT community. As our allies quoted the Bible and spoke using language unique to their roles in the religious community, they were more effectively able to open minds to the possibility that one could be a person of faith and still support LGBT equality.

Overcoming differences was a steeper hurdle. When HRC began this work, most faith traditions did not support full marriage equality. We had to put ourselves in their position to better understand where opportunities existed for agreement. The first way we overcame differences was by finding agreement around the need for hate crimes legislation and efforts to end bullying. We were able to convince some faith leaders that to simply not speak about LGBT issues, or to tone down the rhetoric from such an incendiary level, would be a small victory for us. By doing so, their congregants would trust their judgment to make up their own minds—and in some cases to stay with the church because that conflict was removed. It seemed like small progress at the time, but turning down

the voices of religious leaders in opposition to LGBT equality and adding to the conversation the voices of our religious
allies did a great deal to promote the ideas of LGBT equality
within religious settings and across the country.

OVERCOMING DIFFERENCES MEANS
ACCEPTING OTHERS

Once LGBT men and women felt more comfortable being out
and accepted at work, without fear of reprisal, they were able
to share their private lives with coworkers. As a result, their
colleagues were forced to change their beliefs about gay men
and women—and, consequently, about marriage equality. I
witnessed a change in perception take place before my eyes.
Often invited to corporate settings to speak to LGBT workers, I taught them how changes in corporate policies would
benefit them. During a speech at the Pennsylvania Power and
Light offices in Allentown, Pennsylvania, I noticed that like
many of my recent talks, the audience contained a number of
people who identified themselves as straight, attending out of
curiosity or because they considered themselves allies.

After I spoke, an older straight man came up to tell me
a story I would never forget. His whole life, he said, he had
a distinct point of view about LGBT people. He didn't understand any of it—it just never seemed "right" to him. "I've
worked here for almost thirty years," he said, "and for the
past ten years I've been working next to the same woman.
Last year, she came out to me." The woman had sat at the
desk next to him for a decade, yet he never had any sense of

who she was. When it came to personal matters, they kept to themselves. Every year, Pennsylvania Power and Light was creating a more hospitable environment for their LGBT workers. They added domestic partner benefits long before marriage equality was passed. They celebrated Gay Pride Day. They created a team for the local AIDS Walk. One Monday morning, when this man asked his coworker how her weekend went, she opened up completely. She told him more about the circumstances of her life, including the fact that she was a lesbian. "All this time," she told him, "I never told you because I have been a little bit concerned about how you would react. Now I am less concerned because I am absolutely certain about how this company will react." This company had sent her a very powerful message that her sexual orientation does not matter.

In that moment, this man told me, "I was faced with a massive crisis of consciousness. I had a lifelong point of view about lesbians and I had my point of view about [my colleague]. I had ten years of her being honorable, having my back, and showing me she was a hardworking, salt-of-the-earth person." He realized that he had to make a decision to resolve his feelings about this abstract idea that he'd had about LGBT people. "In that moment," he said, "it wasn't even a close call." This man showed me the powerful unintended consequence of the important work HRC had done in so many of these institutional settings. In this case, making the workplace more inclusive allowed individuals to change the way they felt about themselves and their coworkers. Not only was the company becoming more productive, it was creating an environment in an otherwise conservative industry where people could truly be open about themselves.

GETTING ALONG WITH OTHERS

There will be times when you've done the work to find common ground, whether it's on the personal or professional level, yet the common ground you've found is completely unrelated to the task or project or goal you are working on together. This is especially true if there are significant differences in your perspectives. At this point you have to be willing to exist side-by-side, even though you don't agree. To continue this type of relationship without ratcheting up anger and frustration, take the time to step into the other person's shoes and understand where they are coming from. The truth is, unless you do this work, you are creating an artificial relationship: a saccharin, taciturn agreement that ultimately won't work. Unless you can authentically understand where the other person is coming from, you can't fake putting aside your differences.

This is one of the main reasons why some coalitions fail. When individuals haven't actually overcome the differences between organizations, they can't support each other, even if intellectually they seem to be a good match. For example, there has long been an interesting challenge between organized labor and the LGBT community. Intellectually, it's clear that the LGBT community should stand in solidarity with organized labor, because organized labor has historically supported the LGBT community. But not everyone in the LGBT community supports the premise of unions. Instead of focusing on this difference, I believe these two groups should do a better job of finding common ground, to create a reciprocal relationship that benefits organized labor as much as the LGBT community has benefitted in the past. Sadly, though, the two groups can't seem to get to that authentic place. Many in the LGBT community don't fully understand the common ground that we share: a commitment to social justice and ending workplace inequities. We're fighting for the same things, and we're fighting against the same people; we just can't seem to overcome our differences and work in coalition to support these same goals.

One of the challenges I had at HRC, given my professional background, was working with Republican members of Congress. I'm a pro-choice Democrat and previously worked for an organization (EMILY's List) that had routinely attacked many Republicans for their anti-choice positions. There were an awful lot of Republicans who were willing to support the hate crimes bill, or the employment nondiscrimination act, or even marriage equality, but they still weren't pro-choice; some of them had a conservative ideology that I found disrespectful. However, the work had to be done. The relationship always ended up being more productive when we could both meet halfway on putting aside our differences. Christopher Shays, congressman from Connecticut and one of the sponsors of the Matthew Shepard and James Byrd Jr. Hate Crimes Prevention Act (HCPA), was able to do just that. He harbored a lot of anger toward EMILY's List and the work the organization had done to try to defeat him, but he put that aside. I learned to focus on the work at hand and the common ground we had. I'm sure there were times when we each felt the need to overcompensate. Christopher Shays did a tremendous job of putting aside his differences, and at the end of the day he delivered the Republican votes for us. He did the work necessary to get the bill passed into law. I have a great photo of him, Judy Shepard, and me walking up the Capitol steps on that day.

There's something to be said for standing up for your principles, your values, and staying true to what you believe. I'm not saying that you have to look at every disagreement in a dispassionate way and put all emotions aside at the expense of your self-respect. But sometimes you do have to do this to achieve a common goal, based on your shared humanity with the other side. Once you are through with that process, the achievement of that common win can become the springboard to taking on other areas of disagreement you might have with that person.

:: :: :: ::

Moving beyond your anger to get what you want often involves asking for something in a clear and deliberate way. At this point you're ready to craft the ask. Chapter 5 teaches you how to make a compelling case, how to value your efforts in the workplace, and how to strategically ask for something so that everyone comes out ahead.

5 HOW TO ASK FOR ANYTHING ... AND GET IT

Success comes to those who dare to dream, who see beyond what they have now and imagine a better world for themselves or their community. No matter what you wish for, the reality is, if you want something, you have to make it happen. The days of being rewarded just for showing up are over. In the real world, getting what you want is up to you. In many instances, it involves making "an ask." I'm referring to a proposition about the future: somehow, some way, you want to see change happen. Rather than dreaming about what could be, or what should be, if you really want something, you have to ask for it. The math is simple. If you don't ask for what you want, you're probably not going to get it. This is a difficult pill for the shy among us to swallow, but you probably already realize that the world is a loud one, and those who express their wants and needs usually get them satisfied (unless they are utterly brash and obnoxious, but more on that later).

Also important: the rest of the world cannot read your mind. Most people will not recognize what you want if you don't let them know. If the LGBT community wanted marriage equality but listened to those who said we should focus on other things, sit back and be patient, and wait for the right time for it to happen, we would still be waiting. Just to be clear, while we have always demanded full equality as a community, when it came down to individual conversations with our friends, families, and elected officials, our strategy has always been about asking them to see the circumstances of our lives and to reconsider previously held positions.

If you know what you want and you *don't* ask for it, you are in effect saying "no" to yourself. And when that happens, you are giving permission for others (including your boss, coworker, business partner, or spouse) to say no to you as well. Political commentator Chris Matthews once told graduates at Howard University, "Never, ever, say no to yourself." If deep inside you're saying, *What I'm about to ask for will never happen,* you can't expect anyone else to believe in the dream either. If you don't own what you want—and believe that it should happen—you can't expect anyone else to either. The good news is that you can stop "angst-ing" about how to do it. There is one particular way to ask for anything—a promotion, a concession from a spouse, a meeting with a lobbyist or local politician, or even time off during the busiest quarter—and, almost always, get it. The process is always the same, no matter what the ask is for. It's important to remember that it is a process and that sometimes a dream takes a while to fulfill.

Fighting for LGBT equality taught me that I could ask for anything if I could strategically ask the right people at the right time with the right mind-set. Through planning, process, and patience, I was able to be part of some of the most profound shifts in the American social and political landscape. As this four-step strategy worked for changing the hearts and minds

of millions of Americans with otherwise deeply held traditional views on issues like marriage, I'm pretty sure it can get
you a first date or a better job.

STEP 1: SET YOUR MIND ON SUCCESS

Use your anger as the gift it is—a tool to motivate you to
change your situation, or the situation of others. Once you're
motivated and inspired to think big, make sure that your anger
doesn't pollute the rest of the process, because it might lead to
setting unrealistic expectations. Make sure your intentions
and goals are achievable and not colored by your frustration.
The anger you may feel from being passed over for a promotion might fuel your desire to try in the future for that same
level job. If you let your anger overtake you, however, it can
make you competitive or lose your judgment. If you put the
feeling aside and honestly assess your skills, you'll be able to
see the appropriate next step on the ladder. You might realize
that you were aiming too high or that you didn't have all the
skills needed for that particular job. Make no mistake: there's
nothing wrong with aiming high. Sometimes we have to accept the interim steps needed to achieve those loftier goals,
which can be hard to see if you're holding on to your anger.

STEP 2: DEFINE WHAT YOU REALLY WANT

Whether you're asking for something for yourself or for global
change, you need to know what you're asking for. The truth is,
none of us is as self-aware as we should be. The success of your

ask boils down to knowing exactly what you want, why you want it, and why you deserve it. To figure this out, you need to drill down. Start with the broadest possible goal and work down from there until you can answer these specific questions. After this self-examination, you'll be clear about what you want. Give yourself permission to dream big. Be honest with yourself about what the ask is. If you want something, that want is valid. You have the right to ask for it. Whether you really deserve what you want is another story, and sometimes that is decided by others—namely, your boss, your spouse, a coworker, or an elected official.

Make your ask your own and make it exclusively about you. Don't hang on to a dream based on what other people have achieved. Your dreams and goals should be connected to your talents. This means being able to honestly identify and develop your own *value proposition*—that is, the sum total of what you are currently worth and what you aspire to be. If your goal is to have a weekly meeting with the CEO of your company to share your great ideas (like your boss), you have to decide, given your current stature, if this is a reasonable ask. Why do you want to have this type of meeting? When I was the executive director at EMILY's List, young women fresh out of college would say to me, "I think I would like to have your job, and that I'd be really good at it." I would always say, "Well, listen. There are twenty years between you and me, so if you spend the next twenty years doing what you are supposed to do, then maybe you will have this job."

While it was never my intention to dash their hopes about how long it took me to get where I was, I felt like these young women deserved an honest answer. They would give me this look, as if saying, "What possibly would I have to do for the next twenty that could be as valuable as my Women's Studies major from Smith?" The answer, of course, is living your life and all that you learn along the way. What I thought was logical advice seemed to be staggering news to some of these young women. I would find myself stating the obvious: "There's something to be said for experience. Doing the work is the only way to learn how to actually do the work." Yet I understand that we are living in a world where empowered youth are coming into the workforce armed with new, faster ways of communicating, conveying ideas, and experiencing the world. So why shouldn't they expect to move up the food chain faster?

The truth is, some dreams take time, but many young people don't see it that way. They believe that if they have an idea they should have the opportunity to speak with the CEO about it. But in the business world, that can be an empty desire: there's no good reason this dream should be fulfilled—at least as it's being asked. In other words, wanting the appearance of more stature, or having the opportunity to communicate with people many levels above you, is probably a meaningless desire. These asks are not really what you *should* want. The portfolio of things you should want along your professional trajectory are more money, advancement up the ladder, and a greater sense of workplace satisfaction. Before you ask for something, you have to determine if what you think you want is really what you are asking for. In this example, it's quite likely that you don't actually want to meet with the CEO on a weekly basis. I'm sure you already have plenty of things to do. What you may be looking for is a promotion or an increase in responsibilities that would offer you the opportunity to meet with the CEO.

When you can target what your real dream is, you'll find that there is a sure path toward obtaining it. Your entry-level job might not give you a clear picture of every opportunity within your company. There may be five divisions that report to the CEO, and twenty-five people who report directly to these managers. If your goal is professional advancement—to move within the company to a position of authority—which of these five divisions best suits your skill set and interests? Do you want to go into accounting, finance, communications, HR? By exploring your dream more critically, you've moved yourself from an unobtainable goal to one with real potential. When you phrase your ask the right way, your current manager will be able to see your commitment to the company as well as your long-term plan.

STEP 3: SPLIT A BIG ASK INTO ATTAINABLE GOALS

Some goals can be accomplished with one request; others might require a long-term strategy. "I want a raise," or "I want a better office," or "I want to work more closely with Jim," all require a one-ask plan. However, if you have a super-sized dream (such as "I want to be CEO of the company"), you may have to set realistic expectations as to whether or not that ask can be satisfied all at once. Your big dream can be your guiding light, but you may have to be happy with what you can get along the way.

Smaller, obtainable goals may seem like you are asking for less than you deserve or want. But you are laying down a foundation to eventually get exactly what you want. When I first came to the Human Rights Campaign, repealing the Defense of Marriage Act (DOMA) was something we all desperately wanted, but I didn't believe it would happen for another ten years. We set marriage equality as a long-term goal and started to formulate a plan. We believed that there was a greater likelihood of it happening if we could create a foundation of smaller changes, which for us, meant working to repeal Don't Ask, Don't Tell and passing the Hate Crimes Prevention Act. Our agenda also included strengthening economic and workplace opportunities by passing an Employment Non-Discrimination Act (ENDA) and protecting the welfare of LGBT families in the form of repealing the DOMA and ultimately gaining full marriage equality.

HRC approached these issues as part of a series of things that we actually believed we could get done. Over time, one success lead to another. From this strategy I learned that once you get someone to say "yes" to the first ask, it can inspire them to agree to the next ask with less resistance. When we spoke with members of Congress about these individual issues, we would lay out our broader set of goals. This way they could understand that although we were having a conversation about the hate crimes bill, for example, that ask was part of something bigger. There were plenty of times, however, when the most productive thing to do was to state our business on the immediate issue and get out. The only way we knew which tactic to take was by using these strategies: finding common ground and then listening to and reading the cues of the person across the table. In these instances we made sure that we were all on board with the smaller ask. Asking for something now that is less than what you ultimately want is not coming up short; rather, it charts a meaningful and strategic path to getting you where you ultimately want to be.

When the LGBT community was initially looking to win the right to civil unions for same-sex couples in the late 1990s, there was a lot of talk from our opponents about the fact that it was just a stepping-stone to marriage equality. Civil unions were state laws that recognized same-sex couples as a legal entity but conveyed only a limited number of benefits and protections. These rights fell far short of the wide-ranging set of benefits and protections that heterosexual married couples receive at the federal level, such as transference of social security benefits. At the time most elected officials who supported civil unions did not necessarily support marriage equality. When activists met with legislators, they didn't always focus on the ultimate goal of marriage equality. They won the fight for civil unions in many states across the country and let the victories speak for themselves. The success of same-sex civil unions showed those who were against them that their resistance was fear-based (biblical or otherwise)—and those fears were never realized. Others who thought that civil unions would be enough for same-sex couples were able to see their limitations.

Asking for less is not the same as expecting less in the long run. Achieving smaller obtainable goals allows you to be pragmatic about your larger ones. In other words, if you wanted a twenty-five-thousand-dollar raise and that's what you asked for, because that's what you thought you deserved, and you got a ten-thousand-dollar raise, recognize that ten thousand dollars is not nothing. At the very least, it's a stepping-stone to your larger goal. When we wanted marriage equality and got civil unions, we were still getting something even though we wanted more. Less than what you want is not the end of the conversation. I see it as an invitation to come back and ask again another time. Just ask yourself, *In getting less than I wanted, did I go about it in a way that also strategically laid down a strong foundation for another ask?*

STEP 4: CRAFTING "THE ASK"

The fourth step in this strategy is to construct a plan. Tailor your ask to your specific needs. It's all about the sell, or the pitch. No matter if you are starting with a one-ask plan, or a multi-ask plan, each ask is most successful when you think about it in two parts. The first is to be clear about what it is that you are asking for. If you want a raise, ask for a raise. If you feel disrespected at work and somehow think having a better office will afford you a greater measure of respect, I guarantee you that if you ask for a bigger office, even if you get it, you're not going to get more respect. I can't tell you the number of times people have asked me for something that to them symbolized their achievements but left everyone else scratching their heads. If someone wants a different office and there's one available, I would probably give it to them because it's not for me to try to get at the heart of what they're really looking for. In many instances, as a boss, fulfilling a misguided ask is easy.

A broader statement about your ultimate goals should always accompany your ask. If you're asking for a raise, be clear that you love your job, that you want to be there for a long time, that you believe you have a great deal to offer the company, and that you think the organization as a whole would benefit from your upward trajectory. Don't approach the ask as if it's a negotiation. You are not overbidding; it's not like buying a house. You are not throwing out crazy, pie-in-the-sky requests because you think that you are going to land somewhere lower, where you really want to be. You're not asking for twenty-five-thousand dollars, because you are going to be happy with only ten thousand dollars. You are not asking for marriage with the intention of getting civil union. This is the problem some people had with the Democratic primary platform of Senator Bernie Sanders: many of his asks (such as free college for all and revising the Affordable Care Act) were seen as unrealistic and unattainable responses to the public's anger.

Your ask must be grounded in a way that also directly benefits the other person. It's the rare ask when you request something and get it purely because of the ask. Even if you hit up a friend for a loan, say, twenty dollars, there is the implication that the friend benefits from the ask because the friendship is a benefit to her. Your plan must speak to how the person that you're asking gains from the ask. In the case of repealing Don't Ask, Don't Tell, for example, our ask was grounded in how supporting our agenda would benefit those we had to win over. Remember, many of the legislators didn't care if gay people served in the military or not; they cared about being reelected. To them, our ask was couched in these terms: "According to our polls of your constituents, it would be a good idea if you voted to repeal Don't Ask, Don't Tell. It's what they want you to do, and I know you care deeply about them."

STRATEGIES FOR THE PERSONAL ASK

Get out of the mind-set that asking for something, or asking for someone to give you something, is a charitable act you're hoping someone will simply do for you out of pity or goodwill. An effective personal ask is more transactional; the goal is to make sure you're getting what you deserve while reminding the other person what he or she is getting as well. The same model works in asking for a political contribution. If I am raising money for something I care about and I ask for a hundred dollars, you might hear the ask as if I were asking for a favor. A more effective ask would be: "I know that you care about this issue as much as I do. I'd like you to give a hundred dollars to support this important cause and the good work that I know is so important to you." I have framed it in a transactional way, so you see exactly what you are going to get for your money.

In your work life, a reasonable goal is to ensure that you are receiving a paycheck that is an accurate reflection of the work you provide. Therefore, the goal of this kind of ask is to sell your boss on giving you a raise. Your request must be based on a demonstrated awareness of your workplace's policies. If you know that you are up for a review in February, don't ask for a raise in December. If you just had a review a few months back, don't schedule another conversation "off calendar." You might not realize that businesses have to budget for pay increases; they are not typically given at the manager's whim. Make sure that your value proposition is grounded in who you are and what you've accomplished (and not grounded in any presumptions). Everything else that you say, besides the fact that you want it, is going to be about what your boss stands to gain in exchange for this greater recognition of your work. Demonstrate how your ask is in his or her best interest, so that your boss doesn't retreat, and that there is a willingness to do more. You're not asking someone to give you something; you're not going in on bended knee begging. Instead, you're clearly stating what you believe you deserve.

Your value proposition involves the ability to be honest with yourself, to be completely self-aware in a way that frankly most people aren't. If this is a challenge for you, find the people in your life who can help determine what you do well and what you don't do well. In your particular work setting, ask this person what your strengths and weaknesses are. If you are clear about what you're good at, and what you're not good at, you'll come to the ask from a position of power, because you know what you are contributing and how you can continue to do what you are good at to make an impact in the workplace. You'll also recognize what you might need to change.

If you think you should get a five-thousand-dollar raise, the conversation with your boss should almost exclusively be about what your value proposition was last year and what you have accomplished. This list speaks to the fact that you should get five thousand dollars in exchange for the added value you are likely to contribute in the coming year based on the previous one. Use specific language: "As you know, I've just had my review, and it was rather glowing. I would like to stay here for a long time. Would you consider increasing my salary to X? Here's why I think I'm worth it." The most common mistake occurs when people get into an inequity conversation instead of a transactional ask. For example, they lead the conversation saying, "I want you to give me a five-thousand-dollar raise because there are two other people in the department who started the same day I did and they both make five thousand dollars more a year than I do."

In this instance you have doomed your case. You've reminded the boss that she is currently paying two people, who started on the same day as you, five thousand more than you are and you are forcing her to think about why that is, when she otherwise might not have. There is, I suppose, the outside chance that your boss might say, "Are you kidding me? Wow, what a bookkeeping error." But this never happens. People actually think that the boss doesn't know exactly how much her staff payroll is. Worse, you have not strengthened your case; in fact, you have weakened it. In all likelihood, the boss is now thinking: "The day I moved Pam from $70k to $75k, I knew that (A) she deserved to go from $70k to $75k, and (B) you didn't. I had not really thought about that until now. Thank you for reminding me that the reason I pay Pam more than you is because I think she does a better job."

For a successful personal ask, keep these two pointers in mind:

1. **Keep your list short.** Be clear, concise, and use language that benefits all stakeholders in the conversation. If you want a raise, ask for it. If you want a promotion, ask for that. If you want an office instead of a cubicle, make that clear as well. Your boss can respond to these clear, tangible deliverables. If any one of these are what you want, but instead you hedge by telling your boss (as many people do) that you're bored, unchallenged, not paid as much as a coworker, or that where you sit doesn't fully honor who you are as an employee, your boss will likely be less than enthusiastic, to say the least.

2. **Use each "yes" as a way to build toward the next ask.** This strategy will eventually get you to what you want. You may think you deserve everything you ask for, but your boss, coalition partner, or whomever is the recipient of your ask likely will not. Therefore, if and when you get some portion of what you asked for, walk away with the right attitude— one that isn't angry or disappointed. Instead, demonstrate that you're going to take what you did get and make the case again later that you should get more. When we were fighting for marriage equality, any time we got a tax benefit, a state right, a medical decision-making right, or hospitals to agree to a patient bill of rights that respected the right of a couple or civil unions, we appreciated and celebrated even the smallest victory. These gains meant something to people, so we were always grateful, even though we knew that we had not received all we asked for.

CRAFTING THE ASK THAT BENEFITS ALL

Another type of ask is to request something for the global good, such as a policy change. There is a different progression when you're trying to get somebody to change their mind about something, rather than to give you something. In this instance, you're not necessarily putting forward your own value proposition. Instead, your ask is forcing the other person to recognize your point of view. At work you might notice that a policy could be implemented that would benefit your quality of life. In this case, your ask can be for something that you seek for more than just yourself. It is a much more empowering process—and one that is much more likely to be successful—if you make the case on behalf of everyone. For example, you may be thinking that telecommuting or a change in flextime policy would improve your work-life balance. Consider how these changes might affect everyone else in the office. If they would make the entire office more productive, your ask is for a global policy shift. You'll be viewed as a workplace advocate and less like someone looking to get a benefit beyond what others are entitled to receive.

Asking for a global change involves knowing how the person you are asking is likely to respond. This can mean that before the ask, you need to do the work of developing deep relationships, beginning with identifying common ground. As I mentioned earlier, sometimes in the course of lobbying Congress for various aspects of social change, we would secure one partial commitment at a time. We knew that this was the work of building lasting relationships, which would be seen as the start of a longer conversation. Securing the relationship was something in itself. It was the foundation upon which we based the next ask, and often that was enough to get to the next step. While we were on a fast pace to make change, we had to remember that to these legislators, relationships mattered.

Sometimes, when you are asking for a global change, your ask might not match your ultimate intentions. In the fight for marriage equality, for instance, we often found ourselves operating from a defensive position, where the outward appearance of what we were doing didn't match our agenda. In response to our ask for marriage equality, an effort was undertaken by our congressional opponents to write a prohibition against marriage equality into the Constitution. This challenge was called the Federal Marriage Amendment and, like all Constitutional amendments, the fight began in Congress. Before my arrival at HRC, a Federal Marriage Amendment had been narrowly defeated in the Senate. But now it had resurfaced. Our opponents stated that whether or not the amendment passed, it would be considered an important milestone if the measure received more votes than it had in the previous year.

At the time, Hillary Clinton was serving in the Senate. She believed that the HRC strategy—at least in the context of this particular floor debate—should be to not only win again, but to win by a bigger margin rather than letting our opponents lose by a smaller one. In other words, if their goal was to show that even in defeat their agenda was moving in their direction, our goal should be the same. If we were successful, it would likely ensure that there would be very little appetite to continue bringing up the FMA for a vote. To convince them never to bring it up again was a more important immediate victory than simply winning points on the floor on the merits or the importance of marriage equality generally. Hillary Clinton told me: "If we go to the floor now and talk about marriage, and talk about the hardship that same-sex couples face, and we use it as an educational moment about marriage, we won't increase our vote count. However, if we talk about the fact that we should never amend the Constitution and that Congress shouldn't be intruding on an issue best left to the states, we will pick up some allies."

On the surface her ask sounded like a watered-down argument, which skirted what we thought was an important debate about the significance of marriage equality. Many of our most informed constituents were troubled by this tactic. "You're dancing around marriage," they said. "You're avoiding marriage [equality]." Clinton knew that very few people would be watching these theatrics on CSPAN; nobody watches a procedural vote of the U.S. Senate on a Wednesday afternoon. Americans do not go home from work, turn on their TV, and say, "They're interrupting regularly scheduled programming because there's a vote on the Federal Marriage Amendment or the Keystone pipeline." The Senate floor had rarely been a place where one Senator could sway another with an impassioned floor statement. Hillary Clinton also knew that our opponents were expecting us to take the emotional tack.

Not stepping into that trap, not doing what they would expect us to do, not doing what advocates would want us to do, but doing what bolstered the vote count was all that mattered. Behind the scenes she sold the long game and suggested, "This is not going to become an educational moment about marriage, and if we're going to kill it, let's kill it for good." It's important to ask yourself, *What is for the greater good?*

Another tactic is to look for opportunities or allies that others don't see. In the hard work of creating social change, the strategy often involves a two-pronged approach. You have to work on stopping the bad thing from happening while at the same time advancing the positive aspects of your cause. For instance, when HRC was lobbying to defeat the Federal Marriage Amendment, the Republican congressional leadership was trying to derail us. We crafted an alternative argument, which was that we shouldn't be amending the Constitution to take rights away from people and we shouldn't be trying to federalize an issue (marriage) that was currently a state issue. We would take the emotion out of the conversation and make it a procedural, transactional ask, one that would give some conservative members the political cover to say, "If that's what you're talking about, I'm for that."

The strategy worked. Senator John McCain of Arizona and a handful others walked on to the floor and reflected this very sentiment. In the end, we had achieved our goal of getting more votes than the year before. We got everything we asked for. We were more sophisticated than our opponents thought we would be, and they never brought up the Federal Marriage Amendment again.

DEALING WITH DISAPPOINTMENT

Some people believe that others are holding them back from achieving their dreams. I can't tell you how many times over the years I've heard employees complain when they didn't get what they asked for: "The person directly above me doesn't fully appreciate my talents. He's standing in the way of my advancements." Sometimes, particularly with LGBT employees, women, and people of color, there may be truth to this suspicion. There may be legitimate complaints; there may be some sort of harassment. The best way to judge a situation is to be completely honest with yourself. Ask yourself, *Does my boss not like me because I am a woman? Is he passing me over again for a promotion because I am gay, or because I really don't deserve it?*

Request the unbiased opinions of others to gauge the reality of your situation: think of this as a bit of 360-degree advice. Ask your colleagues to give you an honest assessment of your skills and how they view your status in the office. It's very difficult for somebody to give honest, constructive criticism. It's even more difficult to seek it in the workplace outside of the normal personnel channels. How you set up this ask will make all the difference. You're not going to get an honest response by saying, "I don't know if this is even true, but I think that I didn't get that (raise or whatever) because I think the boss doesn't like me because I'm gay. I mean, I'm just as good as that guy. Well, what do you think? What do you think?"

Instead, you could start the conversation this way: "The best thing that you could do for me right now is be brutally honest, and the best thing I can do is open myself up to receive whatever it is that you have to say. My perception is that I have been passed over because I am gay, and my boss has a particular bias against me. His response was that the other guy was more qualified and did A, B, and C, which merited his getting the raise. And he had some other workplace substance criticism for me. Is that legitimate? I need you to tell me honestly what you think." If you've chosen the right person, they might say, "Okay, Joe, honestly, I don't see it. I don't see him being antigay; I believe his comments are legitimate. I don't think that you do this part of your job as well as others at your level." Hearing this type of truthful feedback can make you more self-aware. Although it might be painful to hear, it's important for your personal growth. Don't let your emotions get the best of you, though. While it's understandable that this information might disappoint you, use these emotions to reflect a bit on the fact that you may be a little disappointed in yourself. Acknowledge the difference between those emotions and being angry with your boss.

How you move past those feelings and clear your mind to determine your next strategic move has everything to do with your ability to succeed. If you can be a mindful listener, and take in what the other person has to say, you will know how to course-correct. The well-intentioned criticism can put you on a fundamentally different course going forward, so that the next time you want to make an ask, you have worked on your weaknesses and can present a better value proposition.

‡ ‡ ‡ ‡

Crafting your ask is often the step to getting what you want. If you're successful, you're done. However, when you make the ask but end up with disappointment and anger, you'll have to recalibrate and create a long-term plan. The ability to stick with your goals, even in the face of adversity, is often just as important as knowing what you want and asking for it. This is called the sheer will strategy, outlined in the next chapter.

6 THE SHEER WILL STRATEGY

Sometimes the most effective strategy is simply to be the last person standing. Whether it's passing legislation, gaining a promotion, or working through a difficult time with a business or personal partner, sometimes you end up getting what you want because you didn't give up when everyone around you did. I'm not advocating simply digging in your heels at the expense of everything else we've talked about so far. You still have to do the rest of the work: build deep relationships by developing common ground, putting aside differences, and developing an ask or value proposition that is meaningful and that you can stand behind. However, sometimes achieving success comes down to simply having more passion for the job at hand than anyone else and finding the ability to draw on that passion in a resourceful and creative way. It also requires an unconditional willingness to try again when you are met with defeat.

The sheer will to get something done when all around you have given up is a quality that can be fueled by your anger; in these moments we understand that anger truly is a gift. This energy force keeps us going but requires constant balance. What separates the people who give up from those who keep going is how they hold their anger. The ones who have the vision and see what's in front of them can say, "I understand what it's going to take, so let's fasten our seat belts and get to work." I call this the *sheer will strategy*. No matter what you want, there will always be obstacles in your way. Problems can arise from other people's best intentions. The sheer will strategy is really about acknowledging these obstacles, accepting the fact that the only way forward is to overcome the complications, and finding the will to do just that despite your anger.

This strategy starts with an honest evaluation of what you want and what's in your way. If you can assess obstacles correctly, you can develop a strategy for dealing with them one at a time. They might be resolved through compromise or simply by the passing of time. Or you might decide that the right thing for you to do is to not compromise, to not take less than you deserve. With patience and perseverance, you can outlast setbacks and move your agenda along.

THE FIGHT FOR MARRIAGE EQUALITY

Mary Bonauto was the first attorney to take on the legal challenges of marriage equality. She brought the case of *Goodridge v. Department of Public Health* to the Massachusetts courts in 2004. Mary was up against enormous odds; not only did she face opposition from those who were completely against marriage equality, she faced significant pushback from the LGBT community as well. At that time, the pervasive belief in the LGBT community was that the American public was not ready to see a marriage equality case brought to court. There was anxiety within the community that if Mary won the case, there would be a nationwide backlash against the LGBT community. Yet she had the will and the fortitude to go against the consensus.

Mary also had a visionary, long-term view, which ultimately proved to be the accurate one. Even though she agreed with the LGBT community's prediction, she understood that the path before us would include soaring victories and devastating loss—three steps forward followed by two steps back. This is in fact the historic way that sweeping social change happened for LGBT equality. There wasn't an easier way and there never would be. So she moved forward. Although there are many heroes and trailblazers in the fight for marriage equality, Mary's sheer will, more than anything else, is what got us where we are today. I once heard her say: "I understand that this case and its aftermath will chart the course for marriage [equality] moving forward. There will be many setbacks, and it will certainly be a decade at least before all LGBT Americans experience full marriage equality." I found this to be a useful way to put the fight into context.

During these early years, I frequently talked about the fact that we were in a marriage decade. The fight would indeed be long and hard, lasting more than ten years. I was surprised, however, when members of the LGBT community criticized this view, diagnosing it as a passive reaction. "Ten years?" was the common refrain. "There must be a better or a faster way forward." As Mary Bonauto predicted, there was a backlash: immediately following the Massachusetts court's decision, thirteen other states passed bans on same-sex marriage. In 2005 only 30 percent of Americans supported marriage equality. Within six years, similar bans were enacted in almost thirty states. For the next few years, the LGBT community was panic-stricken. *Oh my god, this is terrible. What have we done?* Even our allies told us that they were finding marriage equality to be the third rail of American politics. "It's a horrible issue," we heard from them. "It's working against all the other great stuff you've been fighting for, and it's making your allies lose elections." The marriage bans were turning out historic numbers of anti-LGBT voters, who in turn voted against our allies.

Yet had Mary Bonauto listened to the naysayers and not taken that first important step, the rest of what HRC and the LGBT community gained regarding marriage equality would never have happened, including the Supreme Court's 2014 decision to repeal the Defense of Marriage Act (DOMA) and ultimately its 2015 ruling that the denial of full marriage equality was in fact unconstitutional. Appropriately, Mary argued that final case before the Supreme Court; as the fate of the entire LGBT community rested on her shoulders, she drew on that same sheer will.

There were many similar stories over the course of the marriage decade. State by state we fought in the legislature, in the courts, and at the ballot box. We had victories and defeats. When the New York State Legislature first voted for marriage equality in 2009, we lost in a tragic way, only to win the second time around. The first vote occurred at a time when many legislators were unwilling to take a position on marriage equality. They weren't quite for it or felt that to come out in support might be a political liability in their districts, yet they were also smart enough to recognize where public opinion was moving. Many legislators recognized that their legacies might suffer depending on their vote. Many of them said privately that although they were not inclined to support marriage equality, their children (or in some cases their grandchildren) were aghast at the possibility that they might vote against it.

The only solution, in the minds of these legislators, was to simply not bring this issue to a vote. One of the realities about voting in Congress or in a state legislature is that you never bring a vote to the floor without a solid understanding of the outcome. If you watch CSPAN, you'll rarely see a vote taken where everyone is standing around, scratching their heads and saying, "I can't believe we lost." That never happens because the majority whip's job is to know the vote count before they go to the floor. If the whip sees a vote going against the plan, he or she will pull it off the floor. In New York we were at a standoff, until Alan van Capelle, then head of the Empire State Pride Agenda (New York's largest LGBT civil rights organization), and other New York activists agreed that it was time to push for a vote. Our only option was to roll the dice and hope that because of the power of the moment, the strength of the arguments, and the context of history, these legislators would step up and do the right thing.

Yet in December of 2009 we lost: we thought we were poised for a narrow victory, but the final vote count was 38 to 24. The margin of defeat probably would have been smaller, but as is often the case in these situations, once those on the fence see the bill headed for defeat, they see no reason to vote against the ultimate outcome. Either way, we ended up needing to change the vote of at least six senators to be successful the next time. It was heartbreaking. We saw that standing on the right side of history simply wasn't enough. Although this moment might have been characterized as a failure, it was actually an inevitable step that forced the hands of the legislators and caused them to record for history where they stood. In addition, the actual vote provided us with a clear road map to victory next time.

After that vote in 2009, we held a big meeting of HRC supporters in New York. There were many questions about how we should move forward. My message was straightforward: "We lost by six votes. Change the minds of the legislators we think we can. And if we can't, then we'll replace them in the next election. If we do our jobs correctly, there will be another vote after the next election and this time we'll win." The first comment I heard was, "That's the best thing you could come up with?" In other words, a fourth grader could have come up with the same strategy: if somebody doesn't vote the right way, you replace them. The obstacles were in plain sight, but our supporters just couldn't believe that this long-term plan was the only way. They were disappointed and heartbroken, and this path seemed so daunting. The younger volunteers were expecting something more revolutionary, as if there were a transformative speech to be given. But no other path would lead us to the outcome we sought. While expanded efforts coupled with inspirational and amazing speeches that gave people a renewed sense of hope would be necessary, they weren't mutually exclusive to the work I had laid out.

Not surprisingly, there was a degree of anger following the 2009 defeat. I found myself becoming angry as well. The magic wand approach simply wasn't realistic. You know, the one where I come to New York, wave around my magic wand, and *voilà* we have marriage equality. When I checked my own disappointment and fury, however, I knew that what the community needed was reassurance, a reminder that taking the long view would get us where we needed to go. One of the many unsung heroes in that New York fight was Patty Ellis, a member of the HRC steering committee from Long Island. In a quiet moment at the end of the meeting, when it was clear there was not much else to say, she rallied the troops. I can still hear Patty's voice: "Okay. I think we've got it. We all know what we need to do. We have two years to do it; let's go."

Like any other moment of sweeping historic social change, mapping out a long-term plan comes with its own set of challenges. We live in a fast-paced, get-it-done-now, break-all-the-rules world. And sometimes this mind-set creates change. The challenge, though, is knowing which path to take depending on the situation. It's much easier and certainly feels a lot better to follow the lead of the person who tells you that there is an easier, faster way. It's never any fun to be the one who says, in this case, "Nope, there isn't a faster way." When it came to the fight for marriage equality and other measures of LGBT equality, bloggers and critics often latched onto my notion of "the marriage decade." They yearned for someone to simply step forward and speak the words that would change everything: a gay Martin Luther King Jr. But the times were different and the diverse nature of the LGBT community was such that it was highly unlikely that a compelling single voice had the potential to be unifying. If that voice existed, we would have heard from him or her before.

The multitude of voices that mattered in the fight for marriage equality were the couples all across the country telling their stories, helping their friends, neighbors, and elected officials to understand just how important the right to full marriage equality was. Just as was the case in repealing Don't Ask, Don't Tell, the country had to hear from the brave men and women who were serving or had served in silence, and wanted nothing more than to continue to serve their country.

Looking back, the biggest mistake I made was the way I responded to my critics. Instead of responding to the complaints about how long marriage equality was taking, I tried to compel people to just do the work of making the fight take less time. For many, however, my plea was at odds with the anger and frustration they were justifiably feeling. Perhaps my rhetoric might have sounded too much like we were counseling people to be patient; I now understand this was the equivalent to that annoying friend who tells you when you're upset to just relax, that everything will get better. People expected me to express my anger to make a point, to intensify the message to those who had failed us that we would not forget. I was so focused on the daunting path forward and laying out what the next steps would be. In retrospect, I should have shown my own anger more. Simply validating people's passion, frustration, and disappointment could have helped them to understand that I felt it as well. Perhaps that could have had a healing effect and helped people move on to the work ahead.

Two years later, in June 2011, marriage equality prevailed in the New York State Legislature. This victory was one of the great stories of a diverse group of activists simply doing what needed to be done. Day after day they lobbied and campaigned, and slowly but surely they succeeded in changing the minds of legislators or replacing those who had refused to budge to our agenda. While this was one of the final victories I had the opportunity to celebrate during my tenure at the Human Rights Campaign, I've carried lessons from this experience with me in my personal and professional life. Whenever someone expresses anger over something deeply disappointing, and I have already moved on in my head to a solution, I now pause to acknowledge and validate their anger.

LETTING YOUR ANGER OUT

Many people have difficulty taking the long view, and if you are one of them, this strategy may not work for you. Our collective attention span is short. Everybody truly does have their own agenda, and sometimes when they're faced with an obstacle, they may well turn away and say, "This project is too hard" or "I can't figure out a way to get to the other side." The truth is, there is no room for impatience in the sheer will strategy: any type of change takes time and lots of hard work. Sometimes there really is no another way to get what you want than to patiently plod along your course. Often the journey is not glamorous. There were plenty of times during the fight for

LGBT equality when I had to send a team out into the field to knock on doors, pass out leaflets, organize lobby days, make phone calls, and do grassroots organizing. The victory parties were few and far between.

Sometimes, when you look at the obstacles in front of you—all the stuff that stands in the way of getting what you want, all the work it's going to take—it's hard not to think that there must be another way. That is completely understandable, because the path toward victory represents lots of boring, tedious, hard work. Accepting that path, and the work that goes with it, rolling up your sleeves and preparing to do the hard work with your head down for as long as it takes, does not mean that you lack creativity or a revolutionary approach. There will likely be some around you who want to take the course of "burning down the buildings," as I like to call it. Sometimes making a lot of noise, blowing everything up and finding a faster, more out-of-the-box way will work, but usually it won't. Even if that's part of the strategy, it is almost never successful without the hard work that must be done alongside the burning buildings.

The history of the United States is marked by countless fights for social change to expand the rights of marginalized groups. In each of these fights, there have been equal measures of civil discourse and civil disobedience. While both are necessary, the fight won't succeed unless those advancing each effort recognizes the importance of the other. In the fight to repeal Don't Ask, Don't Tell, for example, the final months of work in front of us seemed endless. We had a president who was poised to sign the legislation, had passed the bill successfully through the U.S. House, but faced a Senate where we were six votes short. All of our efforts needed to be focused on these six individuals. This meant endless lobby visits by the brave service members who had selflessly volunteered to do whatever it took. It meant coordinating mass phone calls into congressional offices, writing op-eds in home newspapers, raising money to place ads on television and on the radio. Essentially, we were doing whatever we needed to change these six Senate "no" votes to "yes." We followed the lead of our allies on Capitol Hill and took the direction and cues from the Senators who supported our cause, as they had the greatest insight into what it would take to move their reluctant fellow Senators.

Understandably, many in the LGBT community were nervous and frustrated. The work of repealing Don't Ask, Don't Tell had essentially been going on since the measure had been implemented during President Bill Clinton's first year in office. To many, the work that we had mapped out seemed unremarkable and hinged on closed-door meetings between Senators, a small group of activists, and the White House. Some activists felt that the strategy wasn't transparent enough for the whole community to participate. Yet if we were going to be successful, these tactics mattered; they were central to getting to the vote count we needed. A familiar refrain was: "There must be another, easier way, or one that at the very least makes us all feel better about what we're doing."

Lieutenant Dan Choi, an infantry officer in the U.S. Army, felt strongly that there was another way. A grassroots activist, he had become involved with an organization called Get Equal. They felt strongly that the only way to get us over the finish line in repealing Don't Ask, Don't Tell was to engage in civil disobedience. While I agreed with their overarching argument, I initially felt that big parts of their strategy were misplaced. On separate occasions, Dan and fellow veterans chained themselves to the White House fence, sending a clear message to the president that he wasn't doing enough. The president and our allies in the White House were, quite frankly, confused and annoyed. We were all working together around the clock trying to move six senators, and they couldn't understand why the focus of Dan's actions wasn't instead directed at one of these senators. While Dan's actions got the cause—and himself—a lot of attention, they ultimately caused other challenges. The civil disobedience didn't help us with our allies in the military either; they felt that Dan's behavior, in uniform, was disrespectful. But I also understood that there were so many in the LGBT community who thought, *I don't know if it's a good idea or not, but Dan Choi is making me feel better because he's doing it.*

Over the course of the LGBT rights movement, when we have undertaken civil disobedience that has been well thought out and strategically centered, it has often been the single most important source of progress. During the height of the AIDS epidemic, for example, acts of civil disobedience were used by groups like ACT UP to raise awareness and bring attention to the fact that people were dying and no one was doing anything about it. President Ronald Reagan infamously (and shamefully) refused to say the word "AIDS." Funding for research and care in Congress was non-existent at the time, except for funds that some heroic gay Capitol Hill staff members were able to secretly sneak into bills. Hospitals were turning away dying men. So standing hand in hand across the Brooklyn Bridge, stopping traffic and forcing people to actually see what AIDS looked like was the best and most important thing to do at the time. The actions of ACT UP often looked like chaos from the outside, but there was an unbelievably important strategic center to the organization.

So, yes, sometimes burning down the buildings does work, when it's the right place and the right time. But this strategy rarely stands on its own; it is most successful when it honors and coordinates with all of the important (but perhaps less dramatic) work that goes into creating lasting social and legislative change. There's a big difference between civil disobedience and the search for a quick fix. We would have been happy if any of our battles could have been resolved with a quick fix, but that opportunity never presented itself. For instance, the small victory of getting some religious leaders to leave hateful antigay rhetoric out of their sermons took nearly a decade. We had to map out a broad strategy to reverse discrimination on a micro scale by attacking discrimination in general, with the long-term aim of shifting people's attitudes about gay marriage. Each of these small steps were easier than tackling the large problem and helped illustrate the roadmap to achieving full equality to the LGBT community until we could get everything we wanted.

SETTING GOALS WITH A LONG-TERM VIEW

Where you want to end up, in your career and in your personal life, are your long-term goals. Reaching these milestones requires an honest assessment of what it is going to take to get there as well as a willingness to stick to your plan. When we talk about long-term career and personal goals that can take years or even decades, the sheer will to stay with your plan can be daunting. There will be times when you'll be tempted to switch to an easier path or adjust your sails to what you may feel is a more attainable goal. That will be your decision to make. Quality of life, work-life balance, and how your priorities change over the course of your life may absolutely justify changing your goals. Getting where you want to go simply takes a long time. It requires more steps than you may have initially thought, but do not be deterred. Your greatest regret later in life, if you find yourself in a significantly different place than where you thought you would be, facing the realization that you have not reached your goals, could be because you took what seemed at the time to be a shortcut.

When I worked at EMILY's List, one of my responsibilities was to travel around the country and talk to women about their desire to run for congressional office. These women were business leaders, teachers, lawyers, county commissioners, and small town mayors. My job was to help them formulate a political career path. I would remind them that there were typically two kinds of people who consider a run for political office: those who want the title and those who care about the issues (better schools, the environment, and so on). I found that those who were looking for ways to advance their cause, searching for a bigger platform from which to do this work, were much more likely to be elected than those who simply wanted a political title, even though that goal was much more clearly defined. In other words, people seeking public office are generally much more successful when their goal is to *do* something rather than to *be* something.

For those who expressed a desire to hold public office, I would challenge them on their motivation. I would help them determine what issues they were passionate about and try to tease out a catalyst for their candidacy. Sometimes I was successful and sometimes I wasn't. Inevitably, the candidacies that never got off the ground were the ones who took a look at the timeline and concluded that the time and effort was simply too much. Those who were already committed to doing good work in the name of public service were not afraid of hard work or the difficult path. Although it may have taken ten or twenty years to get there, some of these women—like Claire McCaskill from Missouri and Debbie Stabenow from Michigan—serve in the U.S. Senate today.

The temptations to be driven by what you want to be, how much money you want to make, or which office you want to end up sitting in are a natural part of the human condition. But to be motivated by your passions and what you want to accomplish is not only a more authentic way to pursue your goals, it's also a more successful path. I went to Kansas in 1994 to meet with that state's insurance commissioner, Kathleen Sebelius. She was a dynamic leader, dedicated to public service, well liked and universally respected. There was a lot of talk in national political circles about her running for higher office. I remember talking to Kathleen about a run either for the Senate or for governor of Kansas. Her personal interest was in improving access to healthcare and in the health and welfare of the people of her state. She would run when the time was right, she told me, and would choose the race that offered her the best opportunity to advance her agenda. It wasn't until 2002 that she ran for governor of Kansas—and won. This was no small task for a pro-choice Democratic woman in a state like Kansas. President Obama ultimately chose Kathleen to be his first secretary of Health and Human Services; she served in this role from 2009 to 2014 and was a crucial part of the fight to pass the historic Affordable Care Act.

TAKING THE LONG VIEW OF LIFE

It's human nature to hope for a different, easier path toward advancement in the workplace, but more often than not, there just isn't another way forward. We live in a world where time, information, and career opportunities seem to fly by at a much faster pace, but don't let that reality derail you from the authentic, long-term path you may need to be on. If your goal is to be part of the decision-making inner circle, wherever your inner circle exists, it's going to take time. You'll be included when you have the right level of experience. Looking around your office may offer clues about when that might be. If the inner circle is comprised of people who have been at the company for ten years, that's how long it's going to take. If you've been there for only two years, don't be offended if you are not invited to those meetings any time soon.

A self-aware individual can take that information and think strategically: *Okay, fair enough. My stature at work is not a commentary on me; it's that the value proposition necessary to get into that inner circle is length of service.* So while you might not be willing to sit around for ten years, you can reset your goal to be in a leadership position in six years instead of eight. In the meantime, you will have to double down and work as diligently as you can. Sometimes it feels like the oldest person in the room is almost always the boss. So if you're the youngest person in the room and feeling like the upward path is all about age and length of service, the road ahead of you may seem daunting. The challenge is to balance when you simply accept that fact and when you challenge it. You can successfully challenge the status quo with innovative ideas and a fresh approach to problem solving, not by reminding those above you that the world is changing and being taken over by young people. While that may be true in the most progressive settings, this sentiment is probably not true where you currently find yourself drawing a paycheck.

You may be rolling your eyes as you read this, thinking: *Of course he thinks that way; Joe is one of those old guys. But I'm going to beat the system.* I say go for it. Some millennials may ask, "Why should we be constrained by the nine-to-five work day? Aren't we more creative and more productive when we can be fluid and come and go when we want?" The one who succeeds is always the one who responds: "You're probably right, but if the boss believes that the work day should be 8:30

to 6:00, I'm going to play her game. At least for now." There is a power infrastructure in every office, and it will serve you well to understand it and play by its rules. Get to know the decision makers, then distinguish yourself from the pack. By aligning yourself with the corporate culture, you'll have an easier time making it into the inner circle.

Respect the fact that the forty-five-year-old woman who makes ten times as much money as you do, and is in the position of determining your fate, is never going to say, "Wow. I'm a dope. These young kids in the office are all smarter than me." That's just not how the world works. In fact, the opposite may be true. The older person above you may have his or her own set of insecurities and uncertainties about age and job security; he or she may double down in unflattering views of younger workers based on those insecurities. So why not play the game and follow the guiding philosophy of your boss, even if it appears old-fashioned: be at your desk first thing in the morning, be polite and available, understand what needs to be done to find common ground, and so on. Trust me, when everyone else is railing against these "quaint" constraints of conventional workplace policies, the employee who sees it as a way to find common ground with the boss will be the likely one to advance. However, this doesn't mean you shouldn't also try to be innovative and come up with the best solutions to problems.

At HRC I was the boss; when an important issue came up, I would call in the staff members I felt were best suited to the discussion, without regard for titles or hierarchy. They were my kitchen cabinet. Yet I would hear from people all the time:

"There was a manager's meeting and you forgot to invite me." Their disappointment was revelatory to me. Bosses never forget who is supposed to be included. These are deliberate decisions. Figuring out what's expected of you, and understanding what's important to the workplace, is how you get ahead. Your job is to make sure that when people above you are thinking about those values and qualities they think about you. If the company places a lot of importance on the internal workplace environment, including your interpersonal skills and how you function within a team, and you can demonstrate that those skills are a core and important value to you, you will have branded yourself as someone who is a good fit for any company.

Brand yourself as someone who fits the corporate values by actually exhibiting those specific values. Do it in a way that really shows you're competent in these areas. If it's about being a good team player, then actually be a good team player. The rules may be different if you work in a highly creative or high-tech environment. For example, if you work at a slick startup PR firm, where the work is much more individualized and there's much less importance placed on internal hierarchy, the person who advances is typically the one who is most innovative. If that's the case, that's how you want to brand yourself. If you are the one person in the office the boss goes to if there is a difficult problem that needs to be solved, your branding takes care of itself.

:: ::

Along with having the sheer will to see an action through, there will be times when your intuition is telling you to walk away or at least come up with a different plan. These are the times when you'll need to explore the strategic advantages of compromise and sacrifice. Chapter 7 explores these realities.

7 SACRIFICE VERSUS COMPROMISE

Successful people know when to make a sacrifice or a compromise in order to get the job done. This doesn't mean that they cave under pressure, or that they walk away from their dreams. In many instances, sacrifice and compromise are strategic, productive, and effective ways to get exactly what you want—or close to it. A compromise can be reached only when there is common ground between two parties. When you compromise, there is an understanding that neither party is getting all of what they want, that both parties are giving in a little bit. A sacrifice, however, occurs when only one party takes less than what they originally wanted, recognizing that there is no opportunity to come back to the table again.

As president of the Human Rights Campaign, I had to face one compromise constantly: deciding which candidates HRC would support. A part of our mission was to endorse and financially support congressional candidates who supported LGBT equality. Although that directive seems fairly straightforward, there were occasions when it was not. In these instances, we had to compromise to achieve our broader goals through the legislative process. In 2006, for example, many in the LGBT community felt that the HRC made a major compromise in the face of a broader set of progressive ideals when we endorsed Democratic candidate Bob Casey over incumbent Republican Rick Santorum in the Pennsylvania race for a U.S. Senate seat. While Santorum was arguably the most anti-LGBT member of the Senate, Casey was not fully pro-choice. Historically there had been consideration given in the endorsement process to a candidate's position on reproductive rights. As a public policy matter, both issues are grounded in an individual's right to privacy. As a result of our endorsement, many LGBT pro-choice activists were disappointed in the level of support that we threw behind Casey.

My argument was a simple one. I knew that sometimes, as an organization, we are faced with a choice and have to pick the better candidate, even if he or she is not the perfect candidate. In this case we believed that Casey would be better on LGBT issues, and as a Democrat he would be a reliable vote for Senate Majority Leader Harry Reid. Reid was solidly committed to LGBT equality and would certainly support our agenda on the Senate floor. So, tactically, electing Casey was an important step toward strengthening Reid's power. Casey did in fact beat Santorum by a wide margin in November 2006. Since then, he has been a solid and consistent supporter of LGBT equality. While the Democrats controlled the Senate, Casey was (and remains) an integral player in Reid's army of foot soldiers. He holds the line on Reid's and the Democrats' agenda, including issues he had not personally committed to, such as funding Planned Parenthood.

Two years later, we found ourselves in the position of

supporting incumbent Republican Senator Susan Collins over Democratic challenger Tom Allen in the Maine race. Collins had an exemplary record on LGBT issues—and was a lead sponsor on legislation that was important to the LGBT community. However, she represented another vote for the Republican leadership, who were working diligently against our agenda. Allen, a former member of the U.S. House of Representatives, would have been a perfect vote on our issues. But Collins had stood with us in the past and was immensely popular in Maine. We were caught between the two candidates, but we were particularly sensitive to the message we would be sending to other Republicans if the best we could say to one who had supported our agenda was, "We'll support you until a better candidate comes along." The compromise was strategically successful. Collins won by a wide margin over Allen in 2008 and went on to serve as our lead Republican sponsor for overturning Don't Ask, Don't Tell, delivering an impressive number of Republican senators to vote for the bill.

In these cases, there was certainly anger and some pushback from the rank and file, who believed we had compromised on a broader set of ideals to achieve our long-term legislative goals. I can't argue with them, because that view is probably correct. However, as the leader of HRC, that was my charge. Our mandate was to pass legislation that helped the LGBT community—not to represent any particular political party or be sidelined by a complex set of other issues. The decisions we made were with that goal in mind. So although we may have disappointed some in the LGBT community, the decisions were ultimately ours to make. We couldn't let the fear of that disappointment hold us back from making decisions that allowed us to achieve our biggest goals.

You may find yourself in situations where you must make difficult choices—ones that involve tremendous compromise along the way. What's important to remember is that you, and only you, can determine whether you can make the compromise and see your way to the greater goal. There will likely be other people who have something to say about your decisions, who want to influence your views. My advice is to keep your head down, make your own decisions, and let those around you know it is *your* journey and you answer only to yourself.

COMPROMISE AND THE EMPLOYMENT NON-DISCRIMINATION ACT

It would be nice to say that I had a perfect track record for always getting what I wanted during my years at HRC, but that's not true. One of my greatest compromises occurred when we were working on the Employment Non-Discrimination Act (ENDA). For many in the LGBT community, this compromise was my greatest misstep. My supporters see that the compromise was a difficult decision aimed at ultimately getting us to where we wanted to be; my detractors would say simply that I did the wrong thing. Today, with hindsight and a little distance from the experience, I'm of both minds.

It was 2007 and I had been at HRC for just two years. The Democrats had taken back the House and the Senate in 2006, and at the top of our agenda was passing ENDA. This legislation would guarantee protection for LGBT people from workplace discrimination. At the time it was legal in nearly thirty states to fire someone for being gay or transgender. In states where those protections existed, they often covered only sexual orientation and not gender identity or gender expression. In other words, even at the state level where antidiscrimination laws that covered gays and lesbians existed, those laws didn't cover transgender people. At the federal level, there were no such protections. The Employment Non-Discrimination Bill offered the chance to extend protection nationwide.

Even though the Democrats had taken control of the House and the Senate, and the leadership in both chambers was working on advancing our agenda, President George W. Bush was not exactly on board. The likelihood of any successful legislative effort that protected the LGBT community becoming law was small during his presidency. However, regardless of whether a president is willing to sign your bill into law, it is vitally important to seize the opportunity for Congress to pass a piece of legislation. Taking this action accomplishes many small goals that ultimately help the long-term prospects of passing a bill. For one thing, it's an opportunity to test your ideas and see how they will be received. To have a floor debate, count votes, and see where you are, even if the bill is imperfect, has value.

Another strategic reason to move legislation that doesn't have a chance of being passed into law is to illustrate where the party controlling one body stands in contrast to the party controlling the other. For instance, the Democratically controlled Congress worked hard during the same time period to pass the Lilly Ledbetter Fair Pay Act, despite the fact that

President Bush made it clear he would veto it. Although the bill never had a chance of becoming law during his tenure, it gave Democrats an opportunity to advance their narrative that women should be paid the same as men. President Bush didn't hold this view. Democrats were so successful at driving home this point that this legislation became the first bill passed after President Obama was sworn into office in 2009 and the first legislation he signed as president.

In terms of ENDA, we knew that with our Democratic allies controlling Congress, the time had come to begin moving the bill. Yet as we started to take a serious vote count, we found that there was a significant gap in the support for protecting sexual orientation versus support for protecting gender identity and expression. Many members of Congress didn't want to be put on the spot or on the record with regard to their support for including transgender Americans in the bill, and they simply refused to say how they would vote. Others told activists in public settings that they supported the entire effort, but privately told the whip and members of leadership that they couldn't fully commit. So we had two different sets of reality—both of which were based on a perceived vote count on the floor of the U.S. House—one many activists *believed* to be true, and one some of us *knew* to be true.

As a bill begins to solidify, members of Congress start to pay attention to the particulars. In fact, they pay very little attention to bills until they are headed for a vote. ENDA actually had many details buried inside of the bill. Our allies in the House decided that the most expeditious way to create full support of what we ultimately wanted was to take the bill to the members in parts. Their plan was to first introduce a bill that included only protections regarding sexual orientation, effectively removing protections for transgender people. They would let members study it, ask questions about it, and ultimately commit to it. Their strategy was that by making this compromise, members could get comfortable with what was in front of them, take the bill to the floor and vote on it, and then never have to rethink what they just voted on. Their vote would be recorded so that when we came back for the next vote, we would introduce the same bill yet this time focus solely on ensuring that we had the support we needed for including protections for gender identity and expression.

This same strategy had been successfully implemented for the passage of historic legislation like the Americans with Disabilities Act (ADA) and the Family Medical Leave Act (FMLA). Both bills had been introduced for a vote year after year during the tenures of presidents opposed to signing them into law. Both bills started as legislative efforts that were a far cry from where they ended up. But each year's vote was built on the preceding one, and each time, as members became more comfortable with aspects of the bill as it stood, more protections were added until the bill became the legislation that its supporters could proudly stand behind. So when I was presented with a similar strategy for ENDA, I understood how potentially divisive this compromise could be, but I also knew that this first incomplete bill would never pass into law under President Bush. I agreed with our allies in the House, including Representatives Barney Frank and Debbie Wasserman Schultz. Yet I underestimated the symbolically divisive and painful message this compromise represented. There was a major difference in what we were doing compared with the historical precedents of the ADA and the FMLA. Even though each incarnation of those bills offered more protections for the people these bills set out to protect, they always, from the very beginning, protected everyone. *All* people with disabilities were going to get something right from the start, and *all* families were going to be able to take advantage of some form of leave from the very first version of the FMLA.

Even though it was not at all the intention, the message around the first version of ENDA was that most people would get something but a small group (the transgender community) would be sacrificed for the larger group and consequently get nothing. Although this compromise may have been tactically correct, symbolically it was tremendously damaging to the cohesiveness of the LGBT community. The truth is, the LGBT coalition is a fragile one to begin with. The work of educating the country about the lives and circumstances of transgender Americans has lagged far behind the success we've had in moving the meter of public opinion on a host of issues regarding gays and lesbians. Regarding ENDA, it didn't matter that we were repeatedly saying, "Look, this is not the final product. It is not our intention that this ever becomes a law. We're just using this bill as a way to figure out how to take the next step." This tactical decision caused real damage in the community and sent a chilling message to transgender people, who already felt a tenuous connection to their gay and lesbian brothers and sisters.

Ultimately, the House voted on ENDA, and it passed by

156 :: THE GIFT OF ANGER

a wide margin. The Senate never took it up in that legislative session, and President Bush never had to consider it. Because the Democrats have yet to gain control of both the House and the Senate at the same time, there has been little movement on ENDA. If the Democrats hadn't lost control of Congress in the following election, they would have continued to build on that victory, adding to the legislation each year until we had a fully inclusive bill. The exercise did help bring to light just how much work remains to be done to build support for gender identity and expression on both the state and federal levels. Interestingly, in the absence of a debate around transgender issues, our opponents aggressively attempted to put in place the widest possible range of religious exemptions, allowing people to opt out of complying with these laws and effectively gutting the bill. Today, these same exemptions are coming up in response to marriage equality victories and abortion rights.

THE OHIO COMPROMISE

The 2006 election cycle was important for the Human Rights Campaign because it was the year the Democrats retook control of both the House and the Senate. It was also my first election cycle as the president of HRC. Having come from EMILY's List, one of the most powerful and effective political organizations in the country, I was surprised when some members of Congress—whom I knew from my previous work—talked about HRC as if it wasn't in the same league. While the organization felt inherently empowered, we needed to step up our game in key states to fulfill our agenda.

One of the people I came to know and greatly admire during that first election cycle was Sherrod Brown of Ohio. He had served in the U.S. House of Representatives for fourteen years and was now running for the U.S. Senate. A charismatic leader, Brown is a deeply principled and honorable public official. He also happens to be a shrewd politician and a skilled political strategist. Brown told me that he saw a real strategic discrepancy between the work that many in the LGBT community had been doing and the work that more powerfully perceived organizations were doing. It seemed to him—and ultimately to me—that the LGBT community was working in areas where most members of the LGBT community lived: the progressive areas within urban centers. While there was value in talking to voters in those areas and turning out the vote on Election Day, these areas were already heavily covered by other progressive groups, and the return on the work was not nearly as crucial as it could be in some of the real swing parts of his state and others like it.

Now in fairness, many of the HRC members I spoke with about Brown's comment reminded me that it was central to our agenda to discuss issues of importance in the elections with members of our community, to help educate them about which candidates were true champions on our issues. Therefore, it made perfect sense that LGBT people should canvass potential LGBT voters. Yet I now felt that we needed to do more, that we could compromise from our single-minded position to help someone like Sherrod Brown achieve his goals. If we could demonstrate to candidates like him that we were willing to support their needs as a strategic partner, perhaps they would feel compelled to be a strategic partner with us in the Senate. So we rolled up our sleeves and went to Ohio. Powerful organizations like the Service Employees Union and Planned Parenthood were already working out of warehouses in key swing parts of the state. In some cases they were operating where their members lived; in other instances, they were in areas critical for mobilizing the undecided yet crucial voters. Our HRC volunteers moved into these same communities and went door to door, made phone calls, drove people to the polls, and did whatever else it took to deliver the undecided voting block for Sherrod Brown.

Our message during this outreach was generally broader than just LGBT equality or other issues important to the LGBT community. It was a universally agreed upon message that addressed the concerns of these swing voters—the economy, education, and healthcare. It was a compromise strategy and a message that worked for Sherrod Brown rather than one that specifically addressed our issues. The initial reaction from our volunteers in the field to this compromise was expected. "This isn't what we usually do. We don't know these people," they said. "We've never been to this neighborhood before." But the HRC field team and our leaders in Ohio held tight, telling the volunteers: "Trust us. This is what we need to do."

After the election, when Brown won in 2007, I understood how much this compromise was worth. We had sacrificed nothing. For the first time in more than a decade, we would have the opportunity to advance meaningful legislation in Congress. We would be able to count on more than just our list of "usual suspects" of friends. In order to advance issues of importance to the LGBT community, we would need representatives who were willing to lead, to work with us in strategic partnership, to broker deals on the floor, and ultimately be willing to put it all on the line, knowing that we would have their back. The leadership would ask members like Sherrod Brown, "Do we feel confident that the LGBT community can get our job done as well as theirs?" Now he was able to affirm it: "Well, you can count on HRC; I've seen them do it."

COMPROMISE ISN'T A DIRTY WORD

In today's politically charged, divisive world, the idea of compromise—and certainly sacrifice—carries deeply negative connotations. Hard-line, angry politicians and public figures like Donald Trump have become very good at acknowledging the inherent fear and rage that resides within some people and speaking to them in ways that validate and fuel that anger. One thing people like Trump repeatedly say is that they will never compromise on anything: "We won't give an inch!" They often criticize President Obama for being much too quick to compromise on anything. In some circles, to position yourself as someone completely unwilling to give up anything for the people you represent has come to symbolize strength and determination. Not surprisingly, when these candidates are elected to office, this strategy rarely if ever produces results. Or, I should say, the unwillingness to compromise remains a successful strategy, but the accomplishment of a greater goal never materializes.

For instance, a tactic among some Republicans in Congress

has been to shut down the government rather than allow bills to pass that would appropriate money for things they don't believe in. While they've been successful at actually shutting down the government, these Republicans have rarely been able to sustain that tactic for very long. Yet the gesture and the bravado and, I suppose, the principled stand they are perceived as taking continues to make them extremely popular with their base of supporters, even in the face of failure. While many of us never choose to compromise, we are all called upon to do it every day. Real success, and real leadership, is not at all about a refusal to compromise; rather, it is an understanding of when to compromise and when not to, what to compromise about, and what to stand firm on. When you agree to compromise or make a sacrifice, you have to recognize how it will affect those around you. You have to be strategic about the way you are going to compromise.

Many people are willing to make compromises or even permanently sacrifice some parts of their life in the name of advancing their careers. These compromises are what people are referring to when they talk about work-life balance. You may have to give up a weekend to spend in the office; you may have to give up pursuing a relationship if you have to relocate for a job. Some jobs might make you reconsider personal values or priorities. Your sacrifice could be living in a terrible, expensive apartment, or having to moonlight a second job so that you can afford to act, write, paint, or sing. For many people, being unwilling to sacrifice means spending the rest of your life wondering about and regretting the road not taken.

Let's face it: it's easier to make sacrifices for your career when you're young. Your twenties are the time to put it all on the line, to sacrifice and compromise where necessary and go for it. Most of what you're sacrificing, after all, is a sense of permanence, the putting down of roots either in a home or a relationship. These are all things you can do later in life. The gamble you take in not being certain that those same things will be available to you are part of what you're deciding to give up. You have relatively few responsibilities, and no one worth knowing or working for will ever fault you for using that time in your life to try your hardest. Without the responsibility of a mortgage and kids and plants and a dog, you are in a much less complicated position to make compromises and sacrifices. While it's never too late to follow your dream, it often becomes more difficult the older you get.

I've interviewed many people for jobs whose resumes reflect a huge amount of diversity during their twenties. They've waited tables in New York City, spent time in the Peace Corps, traveled the world, or gone on the road with the circus. Underlying those years and those adventures is usually a story about pursuing a dream. Yet while their list of accomplishments makes for great cocktail party fodder, if they're interviewing with me for a job in politics or social change, they've probably decided that the dream was going to remain just that. Nevertheless, I admire them for having that dream and pursuing it for as long as they did. These early years in your career should be the time to explore your dreams and do whatever it takes to realize them.

I once hired a young woman whose most recent job had been working as a short order cook. When one of my col-

leagues laughingly asked why I thought that was a qualifica-
tion for serving as an assistant to a few people in her department, I said that short order cooks are good at doing many
things at once, they're good listeners, and they're almost
never flustered under pressure. This woman had spent her
early twenties figuring out her life. She had hoped to become
an actress, and although that didn't work out, she had come to
terms with it, and in doing so found a new passion in political
activism. I was proud to hire her and felt a sense of certainty
that she would settle well into this new career path because
she had spent years making compromises and sacrifices along
the way.

THE PRICE OF SACRIFICE

Think about what you're willing to compromise on and when
you're willing to sacrifice. Think about what you are willing
to give up permanently. It's important to remember that your
decisions influence those around you. Giving it all up to pursue a career in acting or working seven days a week to make
partner in a law firm are decisions that you have to evaluate in
terms of how they'll affect you personally. When it comes to
the overall question of work-life balance, however, your calcu-
lation has to take the people around you into consideration.

When I decided to apply for the job as the president of the
Human Rights Campaign, I was single. When I learned that it
was a 24/7 commitment that required travel most weekends, I
evaluated that impact on my life purely in terms of whether I
was willing to sacrifice that loss of personal time and privacy.

What I failed to consider was how that decision would impact my friends and family. I assumed anyone who knew me would respect my decision and see it as the right thing to do. I had many friends who worked on political campaigns right up through the presidential level. In that circle of friends, when someone went off to run for office, or to work on a campaign, we all assumed we wouldn't hear much from that person until after the election. Over a relatively short period of a few months even up to a year, that seemed to be okay for my inner circle.

Yet seven years later, I was still going 24/7. No one should hang their personal satisfaction or happiness entirely on being completely sustained by the work, or the money, or the career advancement. But in the absence of other relationships, it can become easy to do that. You can lose your way. I began to realize that I was missing many of the important special occasions in the lives of my friends. In my mind, I was still off doing important work, but they saw the situation differently. Had I put the work and the cause over the importance of the friendships? Ultimately, those relationships suffered.

I was fortunate, during my time at HRC, to meet the person who would ultimately become my husband. Jed Hastings was a kind, funny, and committed volunteer for us from Minneapolis. We met early on in my tenure and began a long-distance relationship until he moved to Washington, D.C., and we were married in 2010. Among all the wonderful and important things that resulted from that relationship, one of the most important was that I had to reevaluate the professional sacrifices I was willing to make in the context of my spouse and the quality of our lives together. It was an incredible gift to get—the chance to see how wonderful and fulfilling my personal life could be. Together, Jed and I talked about how long I would continue running HRC and when would be the right time for me to leave.

In 2011 we successfully repealed Don't Ask, Don't Tell and had helped to win marriage equality in the state of New York as well as in seven other states. There was a break in the action over that summer during which I assessed HRC's future goals. It would be some time before the next set of big challenges would be in front of the organization, so the time felt right to move on. I announced my decision to leave that September and left the following June of 2012. There's no doubt that I had compromised and in some cases sacrificed a great deal for the work and the cause—and I would do it all over again. Although I occasionally lost sight of what was most important in the context of work-life balance, I find myself now in my private sector role just as fulfilled and sustained in my life and work as I was when I was leading HRC. Every aspect of my life is and was fulfilling, and neither my self-worth nor my identity was ever about my job. This is not to say that giving up the excitement and the energy and the opportunity to work with some amazing people hasn't been a sacrifice, but the memory and the satisfaction of those years remain with me.

∷ ∷ ∷ ∷

It's one thing to be at the top of your game and quite another to use that power as an excuse not to take into consideration the thoughts and ideas of those around you. Effective leaders know that they can't reach their goals alone. In chapter 8 you'll learn about the importance of teamwork through the lens of coalition, and why surrounding yourself with a diversity of opinions makes for a more informed strategic plan. Having a plan everyone can get behind is the absolute best way to get what you want.

8 WORKING TOGETHER TOWARD HOPE

Success can come from individual effort, but more often than not it occurs when people work well together. Throughout the course of your professional life, you will find yourself as part of a team. Sometimes you'll form the team and other times you'll be placed within one. Occasionally, your team will actually be a coalition. A coalition is a group of people or organizations who come together to reach a common goal—even if that goal is not the central or primary goal to each group. For instance, your internal team at work might consist of colleagues, all of whom essentially do the same thing and have the same primary goal. A coalition at work might consist of all the companies who rent space in your building who have come together to talk to the building management about fixing the elevators. It isn't really the primary reason any of you are actually in the building, but it's something you all have in common and want to work on solving together.

Coming together to work in coalition—whether it's to fix the elevators or change the world—has its own share of benefits and challenges. The benefits almost always outweigh the challenges. Power and hope fuels a unique energy when we work in the company of others to create enduring change. The more diverse the group is, the more inspired we can become around a common belief. How you get along with others and work well in a coalition has everything to do with the lessons introduced throughout this book: harnessing your anger to fuel the big-picture struggle, building common ground, putting aside differences and finding common humanity, listening mindfully, appreciating diversity, and recognizing your unique value to the group. How you present yourself as well as your ability to compromise and contribute to the coalition team is equally important, as these abilities will help you navigate your way through relationships and up the professional ladder.

WORKING WITH UNLIKELY ALLIES

The first step is to identify what you require to reach your goals. There will be times when the talent pool you are working with is not enough to get the job done. You might need specialized knowledge, skills, or resources. This is where the strategic work of building coalition begins. Coalitions of like-minded people or organizations put in place to make social change or take on big issues and challenges are easy to identify and assemble. Yet even these types of coalitions are more complex than they may seem. There will always be differences of thought and individual priorities among the ranks, even when you are working toward a clearly stated common goal.

It's important to remember that coalition work can be successful despite a diversity of opinion; teams may come to coalition work representing very different ideas about how to get to the same goal. What ends up uniting the group and creating a unique energy isn't just the shared goal but the shared anger. Figuring out how to tap into that common passion and reminding people of that shared frustration is a good way to keep the work on track and find common ground with one another when it seems difficult. In the fight for LGBT equality, every issue we took on was aided by the formation of a coalition. Some elements of the coalition consisted of the many LGBT organizations and individuals whose purpose was to fight for that issue. For instance, in the fight to repeal Don't Ask, Don't Tell, there were many LGBT organizations whose principle priority was just that. Yet during the fight to pass the hate crimes legislation, the coalition was incredibly diverse, including the Anti-Defamation League, the ACLU, and many labor unions as well as corporations. In the fight for marriage equality, there wasn't just one coalition but a number of them, each with a different focus. For example, there was a coalition of big corporations that supported marriage equality as well as a coalition of religious leaders who supported our views.

While a more homogenous coalition can be effective, the real power and success can come by aligning unconventional allies. When people who normally don't come together decide to stand united around an issue they all have in common and feel strongly about, united in shared anger, it sends a powerful message to others as that coalition brings together diverse skills, contacts, relationships, and points of view about how best to reach the common goal. The power comes from the sheer number of people willing to get behind the issue, particularly if the outside world doesn't typically think these particular groups would work together. The coalition in and of itself sends a united message: "Look how important this issue is. These varied and diverse groups of people are willing to come together." That's the tactical power of a coalition.

A coalition of unlikely allies makes a stronger statement. Other people will take notice, whereas before they might have taken your message for granted. LGBT activists talking about the importance of marriage equality? Of course, they're talking about that. Yet when they are joined by a group of religious leaders espousing same-sex marriage and a bunch of otherwise conservative CEOs, you now have something far more interesting that catches people's attention. For example, let's say your state wants to build a new highway that will run through the middle of town. The community leaders rally to stop this measure. They bring together all of the local environmental groups to form a coalition. While each group is opposed to the expansion of the highway, they all have other priorities. Some care about the forests, others about the birds, and others primarily about the water. This coalition is built around what would be considered as the most likely allies. However, when you ask the small business chamber of commerce to join, who generally never agree with what the environmentalists want, now you are able to take a message of solidarity to the state government: "Take notice, because although we don't agree on much of anything, we *all* agree that you shouldn't build this highway." The coalition unites around the shared issue in a big and powerful way—in an organized way the local community hasn't seen before.

THE THREE-PRONGED APPROACH TO
BUILDING COALITION

There are three concepts you need to be mindful of when working in coalition. The first is to be open to a diverse group of potential partners, then let go of preconceived notions about the individual agendas of these groups. For example, many in the LGBT community were unaware that many labor unions across the country have a social justice agenda and LGBT equality is a part of their mission. In fact, the biggest labor union in the United States, the Service Employees International Union, has been one of the largest contributors to the fight for LGBT equality.

The same is true in both personal and professional settings: evaluate all the potential players, then be creative and resourceful in trying to build the biggest and most powerful group possible. Their commitment to your cause might not initially be obvious, but if they are interested in joining, they will have their reasons. Do your homework, do your research, and be incredibly resourceful and thoughtful about why somebody should be in your coalition. Then be equally resourceful and compelling about selling them on the idea of being in your coalition. Don't leave anyone out because you think they won't be receptive to your cause. In the same way your boss can't read your mind about what you really want (you have to make the case to her in terms of how she benefits by giving you what you want), you may have to help a potential coalition partner understand why and how they might benefit by joining your cause.

There will be times when people are unwilling to join your coalition. Before you move onto the next target, see if you can find out why they were reluctant to join forces. The answer will either help you clarify your ask or help you be more strategic as you move on to your next target. Often in coalition building, you are asking someone to join your cause to achieve a goal that may not be central to their set of goals, so laying out the benefit can be complicated. In the case of the hate crimes coalition, HRC was interested in protecting LGBT Americans from hate-based violence. Some in our coalition didn't specifically focus on LGBT issues but did work to protect other marginalized groups from violence. The time they spent with us in front of elected officials was helpful to us—and ultimately helpful to them as they would be going back in the future to advance their own issues. In some cases, we reminded potential coalition partners that their own members (or employees or customers) would simply view them more favorably if they were able to say that they were championing our cause. In other words, joining a coalition might just be good for their bottom line. If you find that your proposition was not enticing or clear enough, go back to the drawing board and be creative.

The second concept to be mindful of when working in coalition is to acknowledge the transactional nature of coalition work. As you build coalition, you have a moral obligation to lend your support to your new allies at some point in the future. In the LGBT movement we're enthusiastically self-described as having adopted the mantle of the civil rights movement. The imagery and the terminology have been very helpful to us, and we strongly believe that LGBT rights are civil rights. Yet we were not prepared for the reaction from many in the African American community who initially took offense at the way they felt we had co-opted this important language. As I've mentioned, many civil rights leaders have been our greatest advocates in stepping up and making the case that LGBT rights are civil rights and indeed human rights, although the LGBT community had not historically been a supportive part of their coalition. In fairness, that was partially due to how relatively recently most LGBT organizations formed. HRC simply didn't exist in the 1960s. Although early LGBT activists worked for civil rights during that time, it's unclear whether the African American community would have wanted us to be a part of their movement then. After adopting their mantle, we demonstrated common ground in our shared experiences of discrimination and violence. We supported organizations such as the Leadership Conference on Civil Rights and the NAACP. Eventually we succeeded in bringing them into our coalition, and we have benefitted greatly from having so many of the pioneering civil rights leaders stand with us over the past few years.

Don't confuse building a coalition with getting a bunch of your friends to help you move on a Saturday afternoon. Given the choice, I'm sure none of us would help a friend move, but we do it because we are friends. The power of friendship is a very different undertaking than building a coalition, yet people confuse that all the time. This is not to say that you won't make lifelong friends with your coalition partners, but keep in mind the delicate balance that holds the group together.

Understand this transactional dynamic if and when disagreements arise.

The third concept to be mindful of when working in coalition is identifying a power structure among the different organizations when you are coming together around a central issue. Simply put, someone needs to be in charge, and it is usually the person or group who is the biggest in every sense of the word. Often, the person or organization in charge of the coalition has the biggest budget, represents the largest constituency, has the greatest number of personal connections, has the most to gain, has the most knowledge about the issue, and has the best plan. Ideally we should all selflessly work together toward the greater good, but this rarely happens in the world of fighting for enduring social change, and it doesn't happen naturally at work either. Sometimes, more than one person wants to be the leader. In such cases, you can wrestle the mantle of leadership by convincing others that your point of view is going to win. If you think you have the best plan to achieve the goal or solve the problem, you should be in charge, right?

Well, guess what: *everyone thinks that they have the best plan—and almost everyone thinks they should be in charge.* Even if everyone agrees that you have the best plan, you are still going to be competing with the person who has the most money or the biggest army of supporters. So having the best plan isn't enough to propel you to leadership status. You also need the support of others in the coalition. The person with the better plan for achieving success and the ability to bring everyone around to that plan ends up being the leader if and only if everyone else decides so as well. There are many short-cuts you can try on the road to leadership—being the loudest, the most aggressive, or the fastest to run down the hall to your boss's office. But at the end of the day, your ideas and your ability to convince others that your idea is the best will lift you to the top. If you feel strongly that you have the winning strategy, preempt the conversation about leadership by being the first to put your ideas forward. Amazingly enough, sometimes the first idea is seen as the strongest idea.

Identifying a leader is more difficult when you are building coalition between like-minded individuals or organizations. For example, once the many separate LGBT rights groups banded together to try to repeal Don't Ask, Don't Tell, each of the different leaders wanted to control the campaign and the agenda. Some advocated that we be more aggressive on Capitol Hill; others said that we should be more critical of President Obama or that we should deal differently with the military leadership. Yet at HRC we had the biggest budget devoted to the campaign, the largest army of volunteers, and the closest working relationship with the White House. Although many in the coalition didn't like it, it was clear that HRC would lead the strategy and chart the legislative course. This position didn't make us the most popular, but we drove the agenda, put our impressive army of volunteers to work, and spent what we said we would spend. Luckily, our strategy proved successful. When you have a group of unlikely allies, the person leading the group most closely related to the issue at hand should be the leader. In the case of our fight for marriage equality, the coalition included the business community, organized labor, environmentalists, civil rights activists, and women's groups. All of these allies were integral, but everyone understood that this was predominantly an LGBT issue and subsequently the LGBT organizations were in charge and set the agenda.

In each type of coalition, HRC leadership role was the same. We were responsible for both strategy and motivation and with keeping all of our allies engaged in the fight. I understood that ultimately our passion and complete unwillingness to let the issue die would serve as the benchmark for how committed others would be. Being in charge also brings with it a great deal of responsibility for how engaged other coalition members will be. When you fail, by the way, you'll be surprised how quickly reluctant coalition members will be to acknowledge to the rest of the world that you're in charge. Before the real work of the coalition begins, it's important to identify the rest of the players' roles beyond that of the leader. This will be a conversation about responsibilities and expectations, and how each group or individual can contribute with their unique value proposition (what they bring to the table in terms of expertise, finances, volunteers, and so on).

A NEW RAINBOW COALITION

One of the most successful coalitions during my time at HRC was the one formed to pass the Matthew Shepard and James Byrd Jr. Hate Crimes Prevention Act (HCPA). Because the legislation was adding LGBT people to the ranks of other protected classes, it was important that leaders of many of those groups already protected stand with us. Those who had fought to protect women and children, people of color, and those who had been persecuted for their religious beliefs needed to be part of this coalition as well as those who had fought to protect the rights of workers, senior citizens, and anyone else in the United States who had felt the threat of violence simply because of who they were or what they believed. Along with creating a diverse coalition, we needed one that was large enough to achieve our goals. The more people you bring to the table in your coalition, the more influence you have. Many groups came together to pass the hate crimes bill, including the National Education Association, the NAACP, HRC, and the Anti-Defamation League.

Some of these groups were already members of the Leadership Conference on Civil and Human Rights—an incredibly powerful coalition of nearly two hundred organizations, originally founded in 1950 as the Leadership Conference on Civil Rights, to promote and protect the civil and human rights of all Americans. The leader of that organization is a real hero of mine named Wade Henderson. He not only understood the power of coalition, he devoted the resources of his coalition to the work of passing meaningful hate crimes legislation. He and Judy Shepard understood better than anyone else I had the privilege to work with the importance of working in coalition, selflessly setting your own priorities aside for something bigger. On Capitol Hill, some of the newer members of Congress we lobbied saw Wade and me as unlikely allies. They had, perhaps, been visited by civil and human rights leaders and, in some instances, visited separately by LGBT leaders from D.C. and their home districts. But civil rights leaders, LGBT leaders, labor and corporate leaders all coming together to discuss

LGBT issues from their own point of view gave these members of Congress the political cover they were looking for or the language they felt they needed to voice their support back home in their districts. The power of these coalitions helped us to get the HCPA passed. And further victories were always the result of expanding this powerful coalition.

REPLACING ANGER WITH HOPE

After running the largest LGBT civil rights organization for almost a decade, and experiencing as much success as we had, it was no surprise that other lobbying groups and agents of change reached out to HRC for help. Since my tenure, HRC has become the model other organizations have looked toward to create enduring social and legislative change in this country. The immigrants' rights community, reproductive rights groups, the gun control lobby, and others have invited me to work with their leaders, and I've shared the same strategies outlined throughout this book. I strongly believe that if these principles worked for HRC and the LGBT community, they can work for any constituency or individual.

Yet when I read the news, I find myself asking, *Why can't these guys get it right? Why isn't the gun control lobby taking a long view and effectively building a movement? Who is doing the work of finding common ground?* If the sheer will strategy worked for the LGBT constituency, it should work for others. The reason it's not working for other social change agents is that they either haven't fully invested in it, or they are having trouble selling the idea of a long-term plan for building their movement. While there is an enormous degree of justified anger in most of these fights, it seems to me that this passion isn't being used to fuel a productive, long-term strategy. Instead, a hostile reaction to any one particular situation is channeled toward a one-off, short-term solution, like the next election, an upcoming legislative vote, or even prosecuting a particular negligent or aggressive police officer. When these singular efforts are successful, much of the public's anger recedes and so does the collective energy, effectively ending the movement. Worse, if the collective anger is channeled toward one goal and it fails, you've disappointed your constituents who will then have a hard time supporting your efforts in the future. Again, the movement is over.

HRC's agenda was to improve the lives of LGBT Americans first by creating a change in public opinion, so that when we were able to have a vote or bring a case to court, the public was on our side. But this took time and thoughtful preparedness. Changing public opinion on marriage equality alone was a *ten-year effort.* We were able to move from one-third of the country being on board to two-thirds standing with us. We built a movement and identified the organizing principles. We made change wherever we could find an opportunity. The movement understood that we would fail as much as we succeeded, but that there would always be accomplishments (large or small) that would give people hope to stay in the fight. I have the same level of hope for those working in these other movements for change. I hope that they will continue to reach out and find ways to learn from the success of HRC and the LGBT rights movement.

These same lessons will work for individuals, whether you

want to make changes in your office policies or secure your first job. You've learned how to implement strategies and shrewdly negotiate your way into getting whatever it is that you want. I hope that after reading this book, you will look at your work environment in a whole new way. You may be able to spot on the micro-level many of the same situations I've faced. You will find yourself working in teams. You will find yourself working with leaders. You may find yourself wanting to be on a certain career track, maybe in the long term to be a leader. You will begin to discern the different motivations people have for creating their own goals. If you can the find common humanity with that person, you can make the impossible possible.

I hope you've found this advice to be both pragmatic and insightful. These strategies apply not only to the workplace, they apply to the rest of your life. In every personal or professional interaction, you can reboot it by channeling your passion, finding common ground, mindfully listening, overcoming differences, applying the sheer will strategy, skillfully employing compromise or sacrifice, and working together toward hope. These lessons will help you deal with colleagues, friends, and partners in a new, less hostile, more productive way. If you can be curious and use your anger as a gift rather than a curse, you will change the way you communicate, interact, and engage with others. As a result, you'll find that you are happier and better prepared to be a more effective change maker.

ACKNOWLEDGMENTS

This book would not have been possible without the love and support of my husband, Jed Hastings. He keeps me grounded and reminds me what is important in life.

The best advice I've ever gotten about life, love, and happiness has come from my two closest friends, Mary Beth Cahill and Jack Gorman. Their voices and their wisdom fill the pages of this book. I also want to acknowledge and thank my trusted assistant and lifelong friend, Kim Mathis, who has been on this journey with me for well over a decade. For their love and support, I thank my brother, John Solmonese; my sister, Melissa Solmonese; my brother-in-law, Kevin Lonergan; Mary Breslauer and Rebeca Haag; Ted and Amy Gavin; Barry Karas and Bruce Green; Kevin Montgomery and Dennis Durban.

Over the years I've met a handful of people I consider personal heroes. I'm enormously grateful that I can also count them as my friends. Thank you to Dennis and Judy Shepard, Elizabeth Birch, Cecile Richards, Wade Henderson, and Eric Alva. Thank you to the amazing team of people who worked on this book with me, including Pam Liflander, Carol Mann, and everyone at Berrett-Koehler, especially Neal Maillet and Jeevan Sivasubramaniam. To Steven Fisher and Mendes Napoli, thank you for inspiring me to think about writing this book.

I give special acknowledgment to my courageous friends who are part of the Human Rights Campaign family, today led by the brilliant Chad Griffin. Thank you to Vic Basile, David Smith, Allison Herwitt, Cathy Nelson, Chris Speron, Fred Sainz, Harry Knox, Sharon Groves, Anastasia Khoo, Ellen Kahn, Jeoff Lara, and the trailblazers who founded and led this great organization: Edie Cofrin, Mike Berman, Bruce Bastian, and Terry Bean. I'm so grateful to have been inspired by Bishop Gene Robinson, the Reverend Susan Russell, and all of the members of HRC's Religion and Faith Council.

I am grateful for the extraordinary women of EMILY's List: Ellen Malcolm, Sheila O'Connell, Ellen Moran, Karin Johanson, Molly O'Rourke, Jeanne Duncan, Maya Rao, Lisa Robillard, Judi Kantor, Judy Loeb-Goldfein, Sherry Merfish, Shellie Levin, Patricia Williams, Betina Duval, and Anna Lidman. In the White House and on Capitol Hill, I thank Senators Sherrod Brown, Joe Lieberman, Susan Collins, and Tammy Baldwin as well as Leader Nancy Pelosi, Congressman Barney Frank, Governor and Mrs. Michael Dukakis, Jim Messina, Valerie Jarrett, Tina Tchen, and Brian Bond.

To the women who took a chance on me in my first job— Norma Fenochietti, Jean DeVeber and Linda McConchie— thank you.

Finally, I thank my talented friends who generously gave their time and talent to making history for LGBT Americans: Cyndi Lauper, Gregory Lewis, Lisa Barbieri, Meredith Baxter and Nancy Locke, Jesse Tyler Ferguson and Justin Mikita, and Ross Matthews and Salvador Camarena.

INDEX

ABOUT THE AUTHOR

DENIS LARGERON PHOTOGRAPHIE

JOE SOLMONESE served for seven years as the president of the Human Rights Campaign (HRC), the nation's largest gay, lesbian, bisexual, and transgender advocacy organization. Under his leadership, HRC was instrumental in passing the Mathew Shepard and James Byrd Jr. Hate Crimes Prevention Act (HCPA), repealing Don't Ask, Don't Tell (DADT), and passing marriage equality victories in seven states. At HRC, Joe launched the Religion and Faith Program to provide innovative resources for LGBT and supportive people of faith who want to stand up to those who use religion as a weapon of oppression. HRC spearheaded, during Joe's tenure, the All Children–All Families program for adoption and foster care agencies across the United States. The Welcoming Schools initiative provides administrators, educators, and parents/guardians with resources to create welcoming and respectful learning environments for all families. HRC's Healthcare Equality Index rates U.S. healthcare facilities on all policies and practices related to the LGBT community, including patient nondiscrimination, visitation, decision-making, cultural competency training, and employment policies and benefits. In 2011 he was presented with the Hubert Humphrey Civil Rights award by the Leadership Conference on Civil and Human Rights.

Before joining the Human Rights Campaign, Joe spent nearly thirteen years at EMILY's List, one of the nation's largest political action committees. During his final two years with the organization, Joe served as CEO. Under his watch, EMILY's List grew to almost one hundred employees and changed the face of Congress. He is currently the managing director and founding partner of Gavin/Solmonese, advising corporations on organizational effectiveness strategies and policy development and implementation. Joe sits on the national boards for the Planned Parenthood Federation of America and Athlete Ally, an organization that engages with professional and amateur athletes to speak out against bullying.

Berrett–Koehler
Publishers

Berrett-Koehler is an independent publisher dedicated to an ambitious mission: *Creating a World That Works for All*.

We believe that to truly create a better world, action is needed at all levels—individual, organizational, and societal. At the individual level, our publications help people align their lives with their values and with their aspirations for a better world. At the organizational level, our publications promote progressive leadership and management practices, socially responsible approaches to business, and humane and effective organizations. At the societal level, our publications advance social and economic justice, shared prosperity, sustainability, and new solutions to national and global issues.

A major theme of our publications is "Opening Up New Space." Berrett-Koehler titles challenge conventional thinking, introduce new ideas, and foster positive change. Their common quest is changing the underlying beliefs, mindsets, institutions, and structures that keep generating the same cycles of problems, no matter who our leaders are or what improvement programs we adopt.

We strive to practice what we preach—to operate our publishing company in line with the ideas in our books. At the core of our approach is stewardship, which we define as a deep sense of responsibility to administer the company for the benefit of all of our "stakeholder" groups: authors, customers, employees, investors, service providers, and the communities and environment around us.

We are grateful to the thousands of readers, authors, and other friends of the company who consider themselves to be part of the "BK Community." We hope that you, too, will join us in our mission.

A BK Currents Book

This book is part of our BK Currents series. BK Currents books advance social and economic justice by exploring the critical intersections between business and society. Offering a unique combination of thoughtful analysis and progressive alternatives, BK Currents books promote positive change at the national and global levels. To find out more, visit **www.bkconnection.com**.